D0193114

Oxford
School
Spelling,
Punctuation
and # Grammar
Dictionary

HARVEY
RICHARDS

OXFORD
UNIVERSITY PRESS

OXFORD
UNIVERSITY PRESS

Great Clarendon Street, Oxford OX2 6DP

Oxford University Press is a department of the University of Oxford.
It furthers the University's objective of excellence in research, scholarship,
and education by publishing worldwide in

Oxford New York

Auckland Cape Town Dar es Salaam Hong Kong Karachi
Kuala Lumpur Madrid Melbourne Mexico City Nairobi
New Delhi Shanghai Taipei Toronto

With offices in

Argentina Austria Brazil Chile Czech Republic France Greece
Guatemala Hungary Italy Japan Poland Portugal Singapore
South Korea Switzerland Thailand Turkey Ukraine Vietnam

Oxford is a registered trade mark of Oxford University Press
in the UK and in certain other countries

© Oxford University Press 2013

The moral rights of the author have been asserted

Database right Oxford University Press (maker)

First published 2013

All rights reserved. No part of this publication may be reproduced,
stored in a retrieval system, or transmitted, in any form or by any means,
without the prior permission in writing of Oxford University Press, or as
expressly permitted by law, or under terms agreed with the appropriate
reprographics rights organization. Enquiries concerning reproduction
outside the scope of the above should be sent to the Rights Department,
Oxford University Press, at the address above

You must not circulate this book in any other binding or cover
and you must impose this same condition on any acquirer

British Library Cataloguing in Publication Data

Data available

ISBN: 9780 19 274537 8

10 9

Printed in Great Britain by Bell & Bain Ltd, Glasgow

CONTENTS

Introduction 4

Grammar 5-93
word class 5
nouns 5
adjectives 11
verbs 14
voice 38
adverbs 41
adverbials 45
pronouns 47
determiners 52
prepositions 56
conjunctions 58
conjunctions, adverbs, adverbials 60
phrases 61
clauses 63
sentences 66
subject 66
object 69
complement 69
transitivity 70
types of sentences 71
narrative voice 72
effective writing 74
Standard and
non-standard English 76
formal and informal language 78
contractions 82
direct speech and
reported speech 83
Choose your words carefully 85
synonyms and antonyms 86
paragraphs and cohesion 88
correcting your written work 91
proofreading and correcting
work written on a computer 93

Punctuation 94-108
full stops 94
capital letters 94
question marks 96
exclamation marks 96
commas 97
colons 100
semicolons 101
dashes 102
brackets, commas or dashes 102
ellipses 103
hyphens 103
speech marks 104
apostrophes 105
bullet points 107
underlines 108
forward slashes 108
ampersands 108
asterisks 108

Spelling 109–137
vowel sounds 109
plurals 113
present tense 115
past tense 116
comparative and
superlative adjectives 118
adverbs 121
prefixes 122
suffixes 124
apostrophes 128
homophones 130
homographs 131
silent letters 132
more spelling rules 133
Become a better speller 137

Spelling dictionary 138-154

Index 155

Introduction

This dictionary will support secondary level students and teachers with its clear meanings, examples and helpful tips.

In order to communicate well, you need to know about grammar, punctuation and spelling.

This book is full of helpful, easy-to-use information on all these elements to enable you to write well and effectively.

The book is split into three sections: grammar, punctuation and spelling. Each section gives meanings, practical tips and examples throughout. All terms and rules are explained in a simple and accessible way. There is also help on how to avoid the most common errors.

The sections are colour coded to make it easy to refer to any one area quickly, and there is a comprehensive index of all key terms at the back of the book.

The spelling dictionary section is an alphabetical dictionary of over a thousand words that students commonly misspell. These are taken from across the curriculum, including history, maths and science. Support is given to focus on common errors and help you to avoid making everyday mistakes.

The publishers would like to thank the teachers, schools, educational consultants and grammarians whose advice and expertise proved invaluable in the compilation of this book.

Compilers: Jenny Watson and Jane Bradbury
Educational consultant: Geoff Barton
Grammarian: Richard Hudson

Grammar

Grammar is the way that words are used in sentences. Every word in a sentence has a job to do and if the grammar in a sentence is correct, then the meaning will be clear.

Word classes

Words have different purposes in sentences, depending on their **word class** or **part of speech**.

A word can belong to more than one word class, depending on its position and purpose in a sentence.

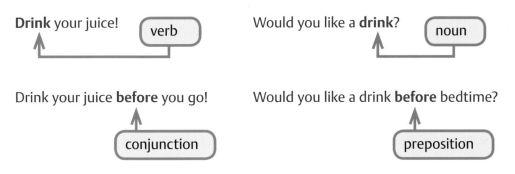

Drink your juice! → verb

Would you like a **drink**? → noun

Drink your juice **before** you go! → conjunction

Would you like a drink **before** bedtime? → preposition

Nouns

Nouns are words like **girl**, **book**, **Mary**, **school**, **year**, **money**, **happiness**. One of their main jobs is to identify a person, place or thing.

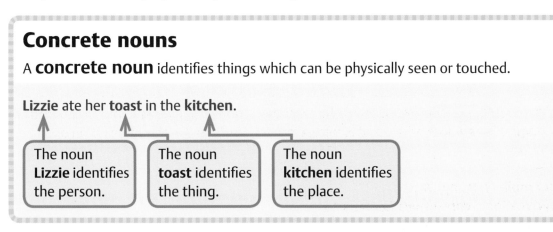

Concrete nouns

A **concrete noun** identifies things which can be physically seen or touched.

Lizzie ate her **toast** in the **kitchen**.

The noun **Lizzie** identifies the person.

The noun **toast** identifies the thing.

The noun **kitchen** identifies the place.

NOUNS

Abstract nouns

An **abstract noun** identifies things which cannot be physically touched or seen, such as a state, idea, process or feeling.

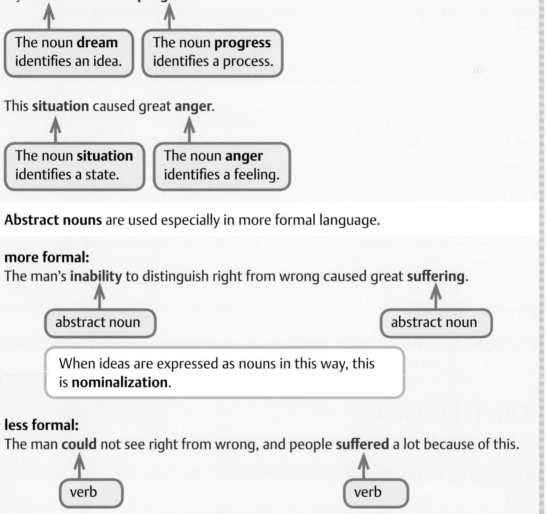

My **dream** is to make **progress**.

> The noun **dream** identifies an idea.

> The noun **progress** identifies a process.

This **situation** caused great **anger**.

> The noun **situation** identifies a state.

> The noun **anger** identifies a feeling.

Abstract nouns are used especially in more formal language.

more formal:
The man's **inability** to distinguish right from wrong caused great **suffering**.

> abstract noun

> abstract noun

> When ideas are expressed as nouns in this way, this is **nominalization**.

less formal:
The man **could** not see right from wrong, and people **suffered** a lot because of this.

> verb

> verb

Proper nouns

A **proper noun** gives the particular name of a specific person, place or organization. Proper nouns begin with capital letters.

James   Africa   **O**xford **U**niversity **P**ress | capital letters |

The names of days and months are also proper nouns.

Common nouns

Nouns that are not proper nouns are called **common nouns**.

organization   continent   boy   day

! Do not use a capital letter for a common noun, unless it occurs at the start of a sentence.

That boy is in the sixth form.

Boys can choose between football and rugby.

! **WATCH OUT**
Some nouns can be proper nouns or common nouns, depending on how they are used.

All the **dads** were invited to take part in the match.

| The word **dads** refers to fathers in general. It is being used as a common noun. |

"I saw **Dad** yesterday," said Laura.

| The word **Dad** is what Laura calls her father. It is being used as a proper noun, just like the name Laura. |

NOUNS

Countable and uncountable nouns

Countable nouns can be made plural. This is usually done by adding **-s**. Most common nouns are countable.

Can you pass me two **slices** of bread?

> The word **slice** is a countable noun because you can count the slices.

Some nouns are **uncountable**. Nouns such as **rice**, **music** and **information** are uncountable. They cannot be made plural.

Could you pass me some **bread**?

> The word **bread** is uncountable; you can say how much (a lot, a little, etc.) but you cannot count it.

! WATCH OUT
Some nouns can be countable or uncountable, depending on how they are used.

a **glass** of water

> The word **glass** is countable as you can have more than one glass of water.

a window made of **glass**

> Here, the word **glass** is being used as an uncountable noun.

Compound nouns

A **compound noun** is a noun made by combining two words.

blackbird	bus stop	pencil case	schooldays	skateboard

Modifying nouns

Sometimes a noun is used before another noun in order to give more information. Nouns used in this way are called **modifying nouns**.

a **soup** spoon	=	a spoon used for eating soup
the **TV** screen	=	the screen in the TV
the **netball** team	=	the team of people who play netball
a **football** player	=	someone who plays football

Recognizing a noun

In some cases, you can recognize that a word is a noun by the way that it ends. For example, words ending in **-ion**, **-ity**, **-ment**, **-ness** and **-ism** are nearly always nouns. Examples include **intention**, **ability**, **requirement**, **fitness** and **optimism**. Endings added to root words are called suffixes.

Noun and verb agreement

In Standard English, when a noun is the subject of a verb, the verb must agree with the noun. This means that if the noun is singular or uncountable, the verb must be singular.

✗ The **match were** fantastic.   ✔ The **match was** fantastic.

✗ **Football are** fantastic   ✔ **Football is** fantastic.

If the noun is plural, the verb must be plural.

Both **matches were** fantastic.

NOUNS

Collective nouns

A **collective noun** refers to a group of people or animals.

audience	committee	class	crew	crowd
family	government	group	team	bunch
pack	pride	gang	flock	

Collective nouns can be followed by either a singular or plural verb.

 His **family was** very friendly.
✔ His **family were** very friendly.

Often the decision about whether to use a singular or plural verb depends on whether you are thinking about the group collectively, or about the individual people.

✔ **The whole team was** staring at the teacher.

> The team is acting as a group so the verb **was** is singular.

✔ **The team were** all staring at the teacher.

> The people in the team were staring so the verb **were** is plural.

 Some nouns have more than one meaning. They may not be collective nouns for all meanings.

For example, the word **class** is not a collective noun when it means **lesson**.

The **class** was about *War Horse*.

The word **class** is a collective noun when it refers to a group of students.

My **class** left early on Tuesday.

Adjectives

Adjectives are words like **big**, **exciting** and **unexpected**. They describe what is named by nouns, noun phrases or pronouns.

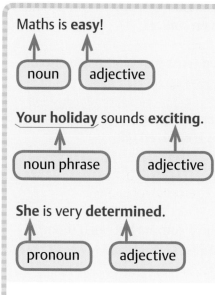

Maths is **easy**!

noun   adjective

Your holiday sounds **exciting**.

noun phrase   adjective

She is very **determined**.

pronoun   adjective

An adjective can be part of a noun phrase.

That was a **big** mistake.

adjective

Everyone loved Mum's **legendary** desserts.

adjective

More than one adjective can be used.

It was a **unique** and **thrilling** experience.
We saw a **big black** cloud approaching.
His actions were **foolish**, **inconsiderate** and **dangerous**.

Recognizing an adjective

In some cases, you can recognize that a word is an adjective by the way that it ends. For example, words ending in the suffixes **-ful**, **-ical**, **-less** and **-ous** are nearly always adjectives. Examples include **joyful**, **political**, **useless** and **dangerous**. These endings are called suffixes. See page 124 for more information on suffixes.

Many words ending in **-ing** (present participles) and **-ed** (past participles) can also be used as adjectives.

an **exciting** day	a **thrilling** ride	an **amusing** trick
a **tired** dog	a **scared** cat	a **treasured** gift

Adjectives and punctuation

When two or more adjectives are used, should there be a comma between them?

The dog slept on Grandpa's **old brown** army blanket.

Here, no commas are used because:

- the adjectives do not have a similar role: **brown** describes colour, but **old** does not
- the word **army** is a modifying noun

His **foolish, inconsiderate** actions led to a fixed-term exclusion.

Here, a comma is used because:

- the adjectives have a similar role: **foolish** and **inconsiderate** both tell you that his actions were bad
- the adjectives could be linked by **and**

His **foolish and inconsiderate** actions...

GRAMMAR

Gradable and non-gradable adjectives

Adjectives can be gradable or non-gradable.

Gradable adjectives can be used after **very** or **extremely**. They have comparative and superlative forms.

It's a **very long** way from London to Glasgow.
The weather has been **extremely cold** today.

Non-gradable adjectives are not usually used after **very** or **extremely**.

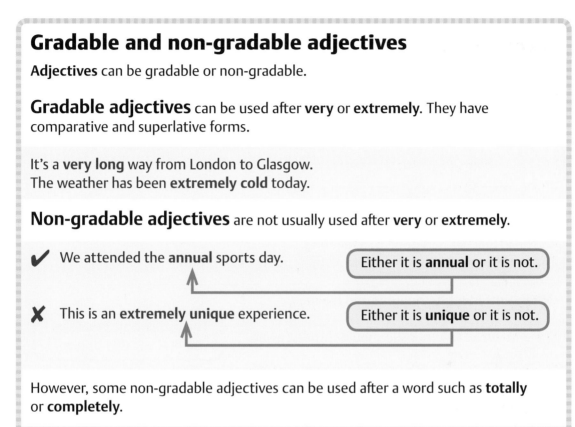

✔ We attended the **annual** sports day.   Either it is **annual** or it is not.

✘ This is an **extremely unique** experience.   Either it is **unique** or it is not.

However, some non-gradable adjectives can be used after a word such as **totally** or **completely**.

✔ This is a **totally unique** experience.

Comparative and superlative adjectives

Comparative adjectives are used when two things are being compared.

Morning break is only fifteen minutes, but the lunch break is **longer**.
My brother finds Maths **more difficult** than English.

Superlative adjectives are used when more than two things are being compared.

The **longest** exam is three hours; all the others only last one or two hours.
This was the **most difficult** thing she had ever done.

For more information on comparative and superlative adjectives see page 118.

VERBS

Verbs

Verbs are words like **see**, **eat**, **sleep**, **sit**, **give**, **think**, **be** or **can**. Some of them identify an action.

Lizzie **ate** her toast.

The verb **ate** tells you what Lizzie did.

The number 10 bus **runs** every twenty minutes.
Tom **finished** his homework just in time.
Year 11 **will be having** an English revision day tomorrow.
The head teacher **had gone** to a meeting.
The Year 9 netball team **have won** all their matches this term.

Other verbs **identify thoughts** and **feelings**.

She **wondered** whether she should throw it away.

The verb **wondered** tells you that she was thinking.

Politicians **are ignoring** these concerns.
Do staff **know** what to do in the event of a fire?
All of the students **enjoyed** the teachers' pantomime.
Unfortunately, this candidate **had** not **understood** the question.

Recognizing a verb

In some cases, you can recognize that a word is a verb by the way that it ends. For example, words ending in **-ify** are nearly always verbs; other verb endings are **-ate** and **-ize**, e.g. **specify, pollinate and fertilize**.

Words ending in the suffixes **-s**, **-ing** and **-ed** may also be verbs. These are verb inflections. See page 17 for more on verb inflections, e.g. chatter**s**, chatter**ing**, chatter**ed**.

Other verbs are used to join the subject of a sentence to a description of it. They are called **link verbs**.

The most common link verbs are:

be   become   get   go   turn   seem   appear   feel   sound   taste   look

The toast **was** hard.

> The verb **was** links the toast to **hard**.

Link verbs are usually followed by a **complement**. The complement tells you more about the subject of the verb and is usually an adjective or adjective phrase, or a noun or noun phrase.

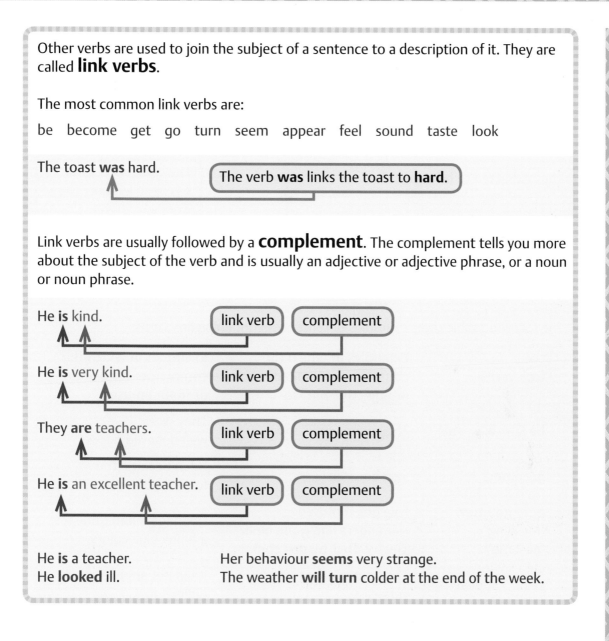

He **is** kind.   link verb   complement

He **is** very kind.   link verb   complement

They **are** teachers.   link verb   complement

He **is** an excellent teacher.   link verb   complement

He **is** a teacher.   Her behaviour **seems** very strange.
He **looked** ill.   The weather **will turn** colder at the end of the week.

VERBS

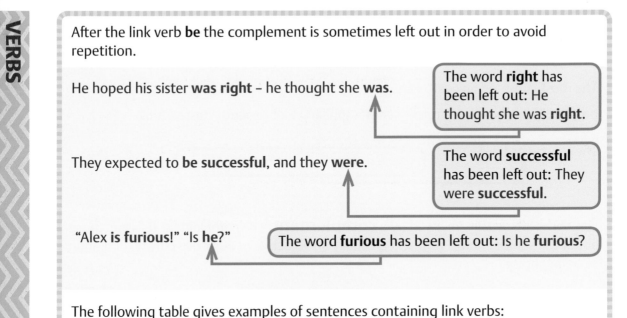

After the link verb **be** the complement is sometimes left out in order to avoid repetition.

He hoped his sister **was right** – he thought she **was**.

The word **right** has been left out: He thought she was **right**.

They expected to **be successful**, and they **were**.

The word **successful** has been left out: They were **successful**.

"Alex **is furious**!" "Is **he**?"

The word **furious** has been left out: Is he **furious**?

The following table gives examples of sentences containing link verbs:

Link verbs	Examples in which the complement is an adjective or adjective phrase	Examples in which the complement is a noun or noun phrase
be (am, was, etc.)	They **were** very happy.	They **were** well-behaved pupils.
become	Josh **became** ill.	Noah **became** the form's sports captain.
get / go / turn (meaning 'become')	Fola **got** confused. Her fingers **had gone** blue. The weather **turned** cold.	Her fingers **had gone** a funny blue colour.
seem / appear	The homework **seemed** very easy.	It did not **appear** a difficult task.
feel / sound / taste / look (how something is perceived)	His mother touched his forehead; he **felt** hot. The muffins **tasted** delicious.	

Verb inflections

Most verbs change when they are used. They may have different endings, or for some, the way you spell them changes even more. They change depending on:

- when something happens (the **tense**)

I **play** football every Saturday.   I **played** football last Saturday.

- who or what does something (the **subject of the verb**)

He **plays** football every Saturday.   They **play** football every day.

- whether the verb is passive or active (the **voice**)

We **play** matches most weekends.   Matches are **played** most weekends.

These changes are called **inflections** and the verb can be said to **inflect**. Verbs can be **regular** or **irregular** in the way that they inflect.

Regular verbs inflect by following the pattern shown in this table:

	-s	-ing	-ed	-ed
play	plays	playing	played	played
Play well!	He usually **plays** well.	He is **playing** well.	He **played** well yesterday.	He has **played** well all season.

imperative

You will **play** well today.

infinitive

simple present tense with he/she/it (third person singular)

present participle

simple past tense

past participle

Matches are **played** on Saturdays.

They **play** well.

simple present tense with I/you/we/they

past participle (passive)

GRAMMAR

The following table gives examples of regular verb inflections:

jump	jumps	jumping	jumped	jumped
rain	rains	raining	rained	rained
wonder	wonders	wondering	wondered	wondered
look	looks	looking	looked	looked
visit	visits	visiting	visited	visited
want	wants	wanting	wanted	wanted

Irregular verbs do not follow the same pattern as regular verbs. Most irregular verbs are only irregular in the simple past tense and in the past participle. Many use the same form for both of them, e.g.

	-s	-ing	irregular form	irregular form
find	finds	finding	**found**	**found**
Find your keys! *imperative* You can **find** your keys first. *infinitive* They usually **find** their keys in their bags. *simple present tense with I/you/we/they*	He usually **finds** his keys in his bag. *simple present tense with he/she/it (third person singular)*	He is **finding** his keys. *present participle*	He **found** his keys yesterday. *simple past tense*	He has **found** his keys. *past participle* The keys were **found**. *past participle (passive)*

However, some irregular verbs use different forms for the simple past tense and past participle.

	-s	-ing	irregular form	irregular form
blow	blows	blowing	**blew**	**blown**
Blow out the candles! ← imperative	He usually **blows** ← out his own candles.	He is **blowing** ← out the candles.	He **blew** ← out his own candles.	He has **blown** ← out the candles.
	simple present tense with he/she/it (third person singular)	present participle	simple past tense	past participle
You can **blow** ← out the candles now! infinitive				The candles were **blown** out by the birthday girl. ↑
They usually **blow** ← out their own candles.	simple present tense with I/you/we/they			past participle (passive)

! Some verb inflections, both regular and irregular, have different spelling rules. These rules are in the spelling section. Here are some examples.

trip	trips	tripping	tripped	tripped
copy	copies	copying	copied	copied
swim	swims	swimming	swam	swum
take	takes	taking	took	taken

Irregular verbs

This table shows the main irregular verbs and how they inflect in Standard English.

imperative / infinitive	simple present tense with he/she/it (third person singular)	present participle	simple past tense	past participle
be	is	being	was/were	been
begin	begins	beginning	began	begun
bend	bends	bending	bent	bent
bite	bites	biting	bit	bitten
blow	blows	blowing	blew	blown
break	breaks	breaking	broke	broken
bring	brings	bringing	brought	brought
build	builds	building	built	built
burst	bursts	bursting	burst	burst
buy	buys	buying	bought	bought
catch	catches	catching	caught	caught
creep	creeps	creeping	crept	crept
dig	digs	digging	dug	dug
do	does	doing	did	done
drink	drinks	drinking	drank	drunk
drive	drives	driving	drove	driven
eat	eats	eating	ate	eaten
feed	feeds	feeding	fed	fed
fight	fights	fighting	fought	fought
find	finds	finding	found	found
fly	flies	flying	flew	flown
forget	forgets	forgetting	forgot	forgotten
get	gets	getting	got	got
give	gives	giving	gave	given
go	goes	going	went	gone
have	has	having	had	had
hear	hears	hearing	heard	heard
hide	hides	hiding	hid	hidden
keep	keeps	keeping	kept	kept

know	knows	knowing	knew	known
lay (put)	lays	laying	laid	laid
lie (down)	lies	lying	lay	lain
lend	lends	lending	lent	lent
make	makes	making	made	made
meet	meets	meeting	met	met
pay	pays	paying	paid	paid
ride	rides	riding	rode	ridden
ring	rings	ringing	rang	rung
rise	rises	rising	rose	risen
run	runs	running	ran	run
say	says	saying	said	said
see	sees	seeing	saw	seen
sell	sells	selling	sold	sold
send	sends	sending	sent	sent
shake	shakes	shaking	shook	shaken
shoot	shoots	shooting	shot	shot
sing	sings	singing	sang	sung
sit	sits	sitting	sat	sat
sleep	sleeps	sleeping	slept	slept
slide	slides	sliding	slid	slid
speak	speaks	speaking	spoke	spoken
spend	spends	spending	spent	spent
steal	steals	stealing	stole	stolen
sweep	sweeps	sweeping	swept	swept
swim	swims	swimming	swam	swum
take	takes	taking	took	taken
teach	teaches	teaching	taught	taught
tear	tears	tearing	tore	torn
tell	tells	telling	told	told
think	thinks	thinking	thought	thought
throw	throws	throwing	threw	thrown
wear	wears	wearing	wore	worn
weep	weeps	weeping	wept	wept
wind	winds	winding	wound	wound
write	writes	writing	wrote	written

The verb 'be' and its inflections

Be is a common irregular verb. Its inflections are very different from the infinitive **be** form.

imperative / infinitive	simple present tense with *he/she/it* (third person singular)	present participle	simple past tense	past participle
be	is	being	was/were	been

Simple present tense:

	singular	plural
first person	I **am** successful.	We **are** successful.
second person	You **are** successful.	You **are** successful.
third person	He **is** successful.	They **are** successful.

Simple past tense:

	singular	plural
first person	I **was** successful.	We **were** successful.
second person	You **were** successful.	You **were** successful.
third person	He **was** successful.	They **were** successful.

GRAMMAR

Auxiliary verbs

The verbs **be**, **do** and **have** can all be used as **auxiliary verbs**. This means that they are used with a main verb. The auxiliary verb helps the main verb to make sense in the sentence.

In these examples, the auxiliary verbs are **be**, **do** and **have** and the main verbs are **work**, **see** and **finish**.

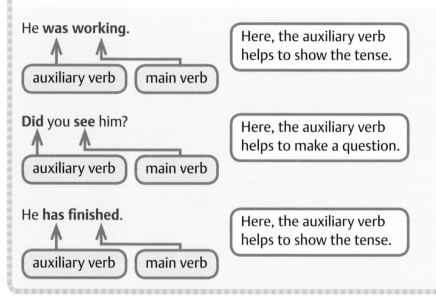

He **was working**.

| auxiliary verb | main verb |

Here, the auxiliary verb helps to show the tense.

Did you **see** him?

| auxiliary verb | main verb |

Here, the auxiliary verb helps to make a question.

He **has finished**.

| auxiliary verb | main verb |

Here, the auxiliary verb helps to show the tense.

The auxiliary verbs **be**, **do** and **have** are used in the following ways.

Be
The auxiliary verb **be** is used:
- in progressive tenses (**be** + **present participle**). See page 30 for more on tenses.

What **are** you **doing**?   I **am tidying** my room.
He has **been working** very hard.   We **were living** in London.
I shall **be working** tomorrow.   I had **been thinking** about him when he rang.

- in passive verbs (**be** + **past participle**). See page 39 for more on the passive.

The record **was broken** by Jean Smith.
This room should **be cleaned** tomorrow.

23

Do

The auxiliary verb **do** is used:

- in questions and in short answers

Do you want to watch this film?	No, I **don't**, thanks.
Did he pass his exams?	Yes, he **did**.

- in negative statements

I **don't** want to watch this film.	He **didn't** pass his exams.

- in negative imperatives

Do not stand on chairs.	**Don't** be silly!

- for emphasis

I **do** want to watch this film.	He **did** pass his exam!

Have

The auxiliary verb **have** is used in perfect tenses (**have** + **past participle** of the main verb).

Have you **watched** this film before?	He **had** already **arrived**.
It **has rained** all night.	They **have trampled** all over the flowers.

 Some verbs are irregular and do not have participles ending in **-ed**. See page 20 for irregular verbs.

She **had thought** of the answer before her turn.

The sea **had swept** everything away.

Modal verbs

Modal verbs are a type of auxiliary verb.

Modal verbs are:

can   could   will   would   may   might   shall   should   must   ought to

Modal verbs are used for expressing:

* possibility, ability or likelihood
can   could   may   might   should

We **could** stay tomorrow.   I **might** help you after school.
He **should** be able to help you.   Tom **can** play the guitar.
Pawel **could** dance really well.
It **may** rain.

* necessity
must   ought to   should

I really **ought to** have revised earlier.
You **should** apply now to do work experience here next year.

* the future
shall   will   would

Araf **will** stay tomorrow.   He said he **would** do it tomorrow.
I **shall** definitely be going on holiday abroad next year.

Modal verbs are used before:

* the infinitive of a main verb   He **might** stay.
* the auxiliary verb **have**   He **might** have stayed.
* the auxiliary verb **be**   He **might** be staying.

GRAMMAR

MODAL VERBS

In negative sentences, the **modal verb** comes before **not**.

He **might not** stay.

Modal verbs do not inflect or change their endings.

Tom **should** stay here now.   Nita and Marc **could** stay there tomorrow.
She **should** have stayed here last night.

In Standard English, modal verbs are not used together.

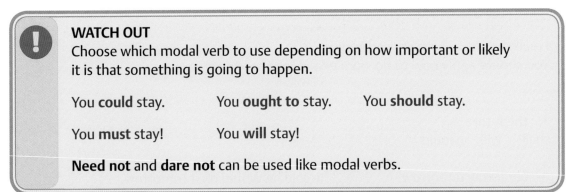

I **can** stay tomorrow.   but   I **will** be able to stay tomorrow.

modal verb   modal verb   Modal verbs are not used together so **be able to** is used instead of the modal verb **can**.

WATCH OUT
Choose which modal verb to use depending on how important or likely it is that something is going to happen.

You **could** stay.   You **ought to** stay.   You **should** stay.

You **must** stay!   You **will** stay!

Need not and **dare not** can be used like modal verbs.

WATCH OUT
Do not add an **-s** to need when it is used without the word **to**.

✗ He **needs** not stay.

✔ He **need** not stay.
✔ He **needs** to leave now.

Phrasal verbs

A **phrasal verb** is an expression using a verb combined with a preposition and/or an adverb. In a phrasal verb, the individual words often do not have their usual meaning.

When you've finished **washing up**, **look after** your brother.

> To **wash up** means to wash the dishes after cooking or eating.

> To **look after** someone means to make sure that nothing bad happens to them.

Other phrasal verbs:

cry off	fall back on	find out	go on about	keep up
put up with	tell off	back down	give out	mess about with

Having a second career plan to **fall back on** is a good idea.
Graham shouted at the kids for **messing about with** the camping equipment.

The phrasal verb **look after** consists of a verb combined with a preposition.

Look after your brother.

The phrasal verb **washed up** consists of a verb combined with an adverb.

He **washed up**, and then tidied the kitchen.

The phrasal verb **put up with** consists of a verb combined with an adverb and a preposition.

I won't **put up with** this behaviour.

In formal writing, you can often replace a phrasal verb with a single word.

phrasal verb	put up with	She won't **put up with** you much longer.
formal	tolerate	She will not **tolerate** you much longer.
phrasal verb	give out	We **gave out** lots of flyers for the party.
formal	distribute	We **distributed** lots of flyers for the party.

GRAMMAR

Finite verbs

A **finite verb** shows the tense. A sentence normally needs at least one finite verb.

I **want** a new phone.   I **wanted** a new phone.

> The verbs **want** and **wanted** are the simple present and past tense.

A **finite verb** agrees with its subject.

Joaquin **wants** a new phone.

> subject   The verb agrees with the subject: it is the third person singular.

Non-finite verbs

A sentence does not need a non-finite verb. Where they are used, non-finite verbs add extra information and do not indicate a particular tense. A non-finite verb does not make sense on its own in a sentence.

✘   **Wanting** a new phone.

However, a non-finite verb may be the only verb in a subordinate clause.

✔   **Wanting a new phone**, Joaquin **called** in to the store on his way home.

> The word **wanting** is a non-finite verb and is part of the subordinate clause.   finite verb

Participles and **infinitives** are non-finite verbs.

Needing a rest from revision, Naz **decided to call** his friend.

> present participle: non-finite verb   finite verb   infinitive: non-finite verb

The present participle

The **present participle** (or **-ing** form) is formed by adding **-ing** to the infinitive of the verb. Some verbs make other changes before adding **-ing**. See page 115 for more on spelling.

needing   thinking   waiting   wanting   dropping   knitting   moving

Present participles are sometimes used as adjectives.

It had been an **exciting** day.
He could tell it was going to be a **boring** film.

Present participles are sometimes used as nouns.

The **meeting** ended at 5 p.m.   There is no doubt that **boxing** is dangerous.

The past participle

For regular verbs, the **past participle** (or **-ed** form) is normally formed by adding **-ed** to the infinitive of the verb. Some regular verbs make other changes before adding **-ed**.

See page 116 for more on spelling.

needed   waited   wanted   dropped   knitted   moved

Past participles are often used as adjectives.

Everyone was very **tired**.
We were all **terrified**!

 Many verbs are irregular and do not have past participles ending in **-ed**. See page 20 for irregular verbs.

She **has bought** some new school shoes.   Ali **has eaten** too much.

The infinitive

The **infinitive** is the root, or base form, of the verb. It often has **to** in front of it.

need   wait   want   drop   knit   move   jump   dance   laugh   swim

Simone intends **to study** Geography at KS4.   There is still a long way **to go**.

The infinitive is used without **to** after modal verbs.

Simone may **study** Geography and History at KS4.

Tenses

By looking at the verb, or verbs, in a sentence you can see:

- when something happens: **present tense**
- when something happened: **past tense**
- when something will happen: **future**

I always **wash** the car at the weekend.

I **am washing** the car now.   **present tense**

I **have washed** the car now.

I **had** already **washed** the car at the weekend.

I **washed** the car yesterday.   **past tense**

I **will/shall wash** the car tomorrow.

I **am going to wash** the car tomorrow.   **future**

I **will/shall have washed** the car before Monday!

GRAMMAR

How do you recognize whether something is past, present or future?
There may be:

• an ending on the verb. The ending is added to the infinitive form of the verb, e.g. **play**, **laugh**, **argue**.

I play**ed** football yesterday.

> The ending **-ed** here tells you that this is the **simple past tense**.

He play**s** football every day.

> The ending **-s** here tells you that this is the **simple present tense** (and that the verb is in the third person singular).

• an auxiliary verb

I **have played** football today.

> The auxiliary verb **have**, together with the past participle, tells you that this is the **present perfect tense**.

Did you play football?

> The auxiliary verb **did** tells you that this is the **simple past tense**.

• a modal verb

He **will** play football tomorrow.

> The modal verb **will** tells you that this is in the future.

• another verb or a phrase

Jack **intends** to play football later.   I **am going to** play football later.

> The verb **intends** and the phrase **am going to** tell you that the playing is in the future.

Present tenses

Simple present tense

The **simple present tense** is used:

• for states (such as feelings or abilities) that are true now

Ira **loves** football and **knows** a lot about it.

• for something that happens often or regularly in the present period

Josh **plays** football every week.   Hollie and Chloe **walk** to school.

• in essays and exam answers about other people's writing

The writer **uses** onomatopoeia such as 'crunch' to illustrate the snow's texture.

The poet's anger **is shown** through the use of several symbols.

It is formed:

• in statements: by adding **-s** to the **infinitive** form of the verb in the **third person singular**

He **plays** football.   The writer **uses** onomatopoeia.
She **waits** here for the bus.

If the verb is not in the third person singular, just use the infinitive form.

They **play** football every week.   His feelings **become** clear.
I **work** here on Saturday mornings.

• in questions and in negative statements: by using the auxiliary verb **do** (or **does**) with the infinitive form

Do they play football?   Jake **does**n't play football.

GRAMMAR

Present progressive tense

The **present progressive tense**, which may also be known as the present continuous tense, is used:

- for something that is happening at this precise moment

Where is Tom? He**'s playing** football in the garden.

- for something that is happening now and continuing over a longer period

This term, Year 10 students **are studying** *Of Mice and Men*.

It is formed with the **simple present tense** of **be** + the **present participle** of the main verb.

He **is playing** football.	I **am waiting**.	**Are** you **listening**?
They **are working**.	She **is feeling** stressed.	

Present perfect tense

The **present perfect tense** is used:

- for something that happened and is still relevant or meaningful now

He **has played** football twice today, and his kit is filthy.

- for something that started happening in the past and is still happening now.

He **has played** for this team for several years.

It is formed with the simple present tense of **have** + the **past participle** or **-ed** form of the main verb.

He **has played** football twice today.	I**'ve played** football twice today.

> **!** Don't forget many verbs are irregular and do not have past participles ending in **-ed**. See page 20 for irregular verbs

She **has bought** a new bag.	I **have eaten** too much cake.

Present perfect progressive tense

The **present perfect progressive tense** is used for something that started happening in the past and is still happening now. This tense may also be known as the present perfect continuous tense.

He **has been playing** for this team for several years.

It is formed with the simple present tense of **have** + **been** + the **present participle** form of the main verb.

He **has been playing** football for years.
We**'ve been coming** to this park since I was little.

Past tenses

Simple past tense

The **simple past tense** is used for something that happened earlier or in the past and is now finished.

He **played** football this afternoon.
He **played** football for a different team last year.

It is formed:

• in statements: by adding **-ed** to the **infinitive** form of regular verbs

play + ed > He **played** football.

> **!** For irregular verbs and their simple past forms, see page 20.

• in questions and in negative statements: by using the auxiliary verb **did** + the **infinitive** form of the main verb

Did you **play** football?   He **did** not **play** football.

GRAMMAR

Past progressive tense

The **past progressive tense** may also be known as the past continous or imperfect tense. It is used:

• for something that was not finished when something else happened

He fell over when he **was playing** football.

• for something that continued for some time

Last term, Year 10 students **were studying** *Of Mice and Men*.

It is formed with the simple past of **be** + the **present participle** of the main verb.

He **was playing** football.   I **was waiting**.   **Were** you **listening**?
They **were working**.   She **was feeling** stressed.

Past perfect tense

The **past perfect tense** is used:

• for something that happened before something else in the past

He **had played** football at the weekend; on Monday he forgot to put his boots back into his P.E. bag.

• for something that started happening in the past and was still happening at a later time

He **had played** for the team for several years.

It is formed with the simple past of **have** + the **past participle** of the main verb.

He **had played** for them for years.   **Had** he **finished** his work when he left?

Past perfect progressive tense

The **past perfect progressive tense** is used for something that started happening in the past and was still happening at a later time. It may also be known as the past perfect continuous tense.

He **had been playing** for the team for several years.

It is formed with the simple past of **have** + **been** + the **present participle** of the main verb.

My cousin **had been coming** to visit every year.
We **had been meeting** for lunch every day.

WATCH OUT
Past tenses are also used when talking about something that might happen, or something that you would like to be true.

If he **played** for a different team, he might get more matches.
I wish I still **played** football.   If only I **had remembered** my phone!

Future

To show that something will definitely, or most probably, happen in the **future** you can use one of the following:

- the modal verb **will** + the **infinitive** of the main verb

He **will play** football this evening.   **Will** you **learn** your spellings later?

- the modal verb **shall** + the **infinitive** of the main verb, especially in the first person

I **shall play** football this evening.

! Watch out! In conversation and informal writing, **will** and **shall** are often contracted.

He**'ll** play football tomorrow.   I**'ll** play football tomorrow.

- another verb or phrase that expresses intention or desire

I **am going to** play football later.   Beth **wants to** finish her homework after tea.

intention   desire

Tim **intends to** train as an accountant.   I **would like to** learn Japanese.

intention   desire

- Other phrases that suggest something will happen include:

be about to do something   **be on the point of** doing something
be on the verge of doing something

The head teacher **is about to** announce the results.

- If something is less certain to happen, you can use the modal verb **might** or **may**.

We **might** go swimming later.   Mr Smith **may** arrive late; he is off-site with Year 9.

FUTURE

Future time is also shown by using a present tense or the modal **can**.

He is **staying** here tomorrow night.   You **can** do it later.
We **leave** at 5 p.m. tomorrow.   He **can** stay here.
The train **arrives** tomorrow evening.   **Can** you walk our dog when we're away?

Active and passive voice

Many verbs can be either **active** or **passive**.

The sentence below has an **active** verb.

Peter cleans his bedroom every week.

The words **his bedroom** are the object of the verb.

The word **cleans** is the verb.

Peter is the subject of the verb.

With an **active** verb, the subject is often who or what does something. Here, Peter is the person who is cleaning his room.

Compare the sentence above with the one following, which has a **passive** verb.

Peter's bedroom is cleaned every week.

The words **is cleaned** form the passive verb.

Peter's bedroom is the subject of the verb.

With a passive verb, the subject is the person or thing that would have been the object if the verb had been active. Here, the bedroom is cleaned but we do not know who does it.

GRAMMAR

Use a passive verb:

- to focus on what happens, rather than on who does something

Matches are played every weekend.

The sentence begins with **Matches are played**... as this is the focus of the sentence, rather than who plays the matches.

The anger is shown most clearly in the last stanza.

The sentence begins with **The anger is shown**. This is the focus of the sentence rather than who shows the anger.

- to speak and write more formally

The issue **was dealt with** as rapidly as possible.

> This sounds more formal than **We dealt with the issue, People dealt with the issue** or **They dealt with the issue.**

- when it is convenient to name the person affected as the subject, followed by the person who did the action (the do-er) after the word **by**.

Susan applied for the job and **was interviewed by the manager** on Tuesday.

> Susan is now the subject of **applied** and **was interviewed**.

> Here, **the manager** is the do-er and follows the word **by**.

GRAMMAR

Make a verb passive by using the auxiliary verb **be** + the **past participle** of the main verb.

His room **is cleaned** every week.   All the food **had been eaten**.

If you want to say **who** does something (the do-er), use an adverbial starting with **by**:

All the food had been eaten **by the teachers**!

If you want to say **how**, **when** or **where** something is done, you can also use an adverbial.

The poet's anger **is shown** most clearly **in the last stanza.**

passive   adverbial

WATCH OUT
You can use a passive verb in any tense.
Last year, matches **were played** on Wednesday evenings.
This year, matches **are played** on Saturdays.
Next year, matches **will be played** on Sundays.

Adverbs

Adverbs are used to modify verbs, adjectives, other adverbs or whole sentences.

Some **adverbs** answer questions starting **How...?** or **In what way...?**
These are **adverbs of manner**.

She listened **carefully** to what he said.   It was **strangely** quiet.

Some adverbs answer questions starting **When..?** These are **adverbs of time**.

I'll see you **tomorrow**.   We had finished the work **earlier**.

Some **adverbs** answer questions starting **How often...?**
These are **adverbs of frequency**.

Sometimes we have pizza for tea.   They **often** had arguments.

Some **adverbs** answer questions starting **How much...?** or **To what extent...?**
These are **adverbs of degree**.

We **really** tried our best, but the other team was better.   He felt **extremely** upset.

Some **adverbs** answer questions starting **Where..?** These are **adverbs of place**.

We looked **everywhere**.   Erica came **downstairs**.

Some **adverbs** add a comment about the event or about its likelihood.

We **definitely** should have won!   **Perhaps** he forgot.
Unfortunately, the referee seemed to have a blind spot.

Some **adverbs** are **cohesive devices** (and may be known as connectives).

Doctors earn a great deal of money. **However**, they have a great deal of responsibility.

More examples:

afterwards	again	also	beforehand	elsewhere	eventually
finally	furthermore	however	later	moreover	nevertheless
next	nonetheless	overall	soon	therefore	otherwise

Adverbs can modify a **verb**.

Lizzie chewed **slowly**.

> The adverb **slowly** tells you how Lizzie chewed.

Adverbs can modify an **adjective**.

Lizzie's toast was **unpleasantly** hard.

> The adverb **unpleasantly** gives you more information about the way in which the toast was hard.

Lizzie's toast was **really** hard.

> The adverb **really** tells you how hard the toast was.

Adverbs can modify another **adverb**.

Lizzie chewed **very** slowly.

> The adverb **very** tells you how slowly Lizzie chewed.

The adverbs **really** and **very** are sometimes called **intensifiers** or **emphasizers**: they intensify, or emphasize, an adjective or another adverb.

Adverbs like this include:

extremely   really   so   terribly   too   very   completely   totally   utterly

We are **extremely** sorry that you were not satisfied with our product.

GRAMMAR

The adverb **quite** can mean 'completely'.

That's **quite** brilliant!

It can also mean 'to some extent, but not very'.

That cake is **quite** good, but I prefer the other one.

Other words that mean 'to some extent, but not very' include **fairly** and **relatively**.

The first question was **relatively** easy.

Some adverbs can modify a whole sentence.

Not **surprisingly**, Lizzie was unable to swallow the toast.
Unfortunately, our dog died last week.

Adverbs that are used in this way are sometimes called **sentence adverbs**. Some sentence adverbs are **cohesive**: examples include **however**, **moreover** and **nevertheless**.

Much progress has been made. **Nevertheless**, we must not become complacent.

The adverbs **always** and **never** are usually used between the subject and the verb.

He **always** played football on Saturdays.   I **never** enjoy athletics.

! **WATCH OUT**
In formal writing, avoid starting sentences with **Also**. Your writing will flow more elegantly if you insert **also** before the main verb.

The government **also faced** the problem of rising food prices.
The writer **may also intend** to make the reader think about justice.

GRAMMAR

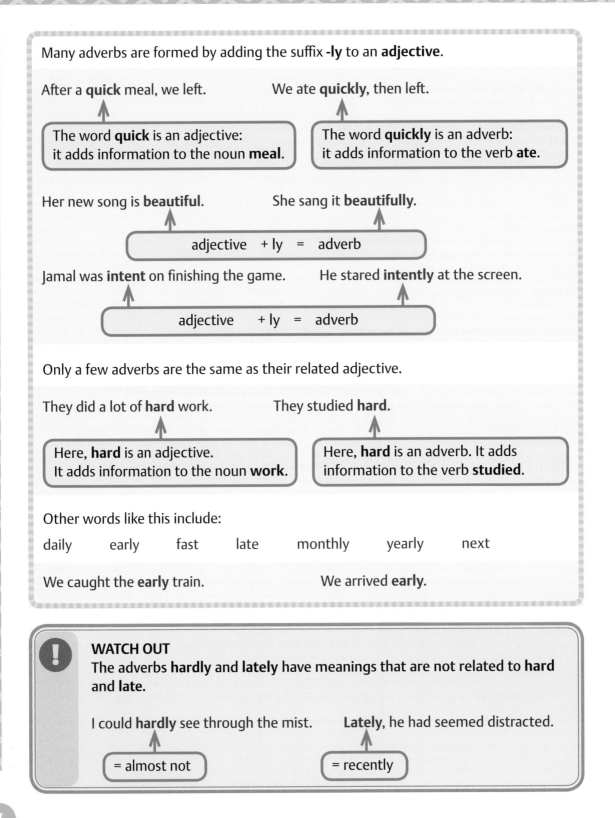

Many adverbs are formed by adding the suffix **-ly** to an **adjective**.

After a **quick** meal, we left.　　　We ate **quickly**, then left.

The word **quick** is an adjective: it adds information to the noun **meal**.

The word **quickly** is an adverb: it adds information to the verb **ate**.

Her new song is **beautiful**.　　　She sang it **beautifully**.

adjective　+ ly　=　adverb

Jamal was **intent** on finishing the game.　　He stared **intently** at the screen.

adjective　+ ly　=　adverb

Only a few adverbs are the same as their related adjective.

They did a lot of **hard** work.　　　They studied **hard**.

Here, **hard** is an adjective. It adds information to the noun **work**.

Here, **hard** is an adverb. It adds information to the verb **studied**.

Other words like this include:

daily　　early　　fast　　late　　monthly　　yearly　　next

We caught the **early** train.　　　　We arrived **early**.

> **!** **WATCH OUT**
> The adverbs **hardly** and **lately** have meanings that are not related to **hard** and **late**.
>
> I could **hardly** see through the mist.　　**Lately**, he had seemed distracted.
>
> = almost not　　　　　　　= recently

Adverbials

An **adverbial** is an adverb, phrase or clause that modifies a verb.

We saw him **recently**.
We saw him **in the evening**.

We saw him **last night**.
We saw him **when he came to visit**.

Some **adverbials** answer questions starting **When...?** or **How often...?** or **For how long...?**

I need to be back home **at 8 p.m.**
They went on holiday **yesterday afternoon**.
She wished she could be on holiday **every week**.
The cat sleeps **all day**.

Some **adverbials** answer questions starting **How much...?** or **To what extent...?**

He worked **very hard**.
Joanna said she had **more or less** finished her art folder.

Some **adverbials** answer questions starting **How...?** or **In what way...?**

She stood **with her head bent to one side**.
The writer's feelings are seen **in the words 'laugh' and 'joyful'**.

Some **adverbials** answer questions starting **Where...?**

The dog slept **under the table**.

Some **adverbials** answer questions starting **Why...?** or **For what purpose...?**

Everyone had arrived **for the meeting**.
Mum packed a shovel in the boot of the car **in case it snowed**.

ADVERBIALS

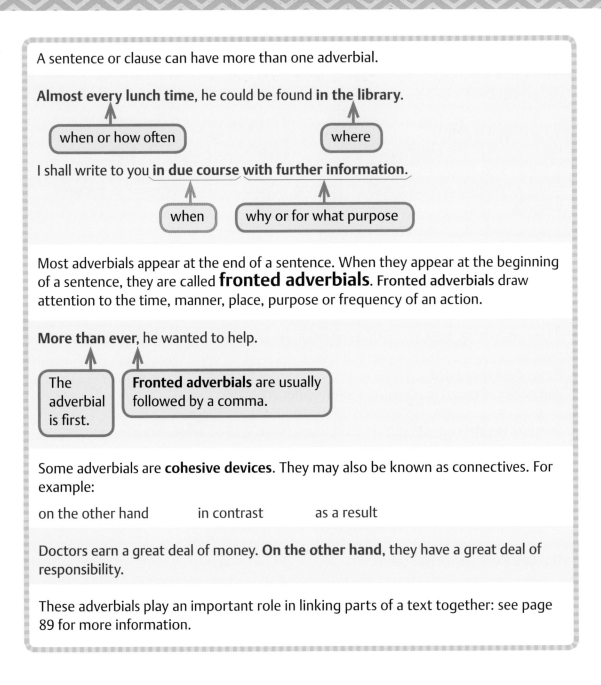

A sentence or clause can have more than one adverbial.

Almost every lunch time, he could be found **in the library**.

when or how often

where

I shall write to you **in due course** **with further information**.

when

why or for what purpose

Most adverbials appear at the end of a sentence. When they appear at the beginning of a sentence, they are called **fronted adverbials**. Fronted adverbials draw attention to the time, manner, place, purpose or frequency of an action.

More than ever, he wanted to help.

The adverbial is first.

Fronted adverbials are usually followed by a comma.

Some adverbials are **cohesive devices**. They may also be known as connectives. For example:

on the other hand   in contrast   as a result

Doctors earn a great deal of money. **On the other hand**, they have a great deal of responsibility.

These adverbials play an important role in linking parts of a text together: see page 89 for more information.

Pronouns

Pronouns are words like **me**, **herself**, **yours**, **this**, **who**, **no one** or **everything**. Pronouns can be used instead of nouns or noun phrases.

Personal pronouns refer to people or things that are already known.

Mr Smith saw Lucy using a phone; thinking **she** was a student, **he** tried to confiscate **it**!

The pronoun **it** refers to the **phone**.

The pronoun **she** refers to **Lucy**.

The pronoun **he** refers to **Mr Smith**.

Most personal pronouns have different forms, depending on whether they are the **subject** of the verb or the **object** of the verb:

	singular	plural
first person	subject: I object: me	subject: we object: us
second person	subject: you object: you	subject: you object: you
third person	subject: he, she or it object: him, her or it	subject: they object: them

The old man smiled at his granddaughter. **He** patted **her** on the head.

subject of the verb (the do-er, doing the action)

object of the verb (on the receiving end of the action)

Possessive pronouns tell you who owns the thing you are talking about or who is involved in the process or action.

Lucy was using a phone. It was **hers**.

> The pronoun **hers** tells you that the phone belonged to Lucy.

"Mum, I've lost my shoes! Please can I borrow **yours**?" yelled Lizzie.

> The pronoun **yours** tells you that the shoes belonged to Lizzie's mum.

Rob told Mrs Smith that the decision had been **his**.

> The pronoun **his** tells you that it was Rob's decision.

The following table gives the possessive pronouns used in this way.

	singular	plural
first person	mine	ours
second person	yours	yours
third person	his, hers or its (The possessive pronoun its is rarely used.)	theirs

WATCH OUT

It is easy to confuse possessive pronouns with possessive determiners. Possessive pronouns are used instead of the noun. Possessive determiners are used with a noun, to show who or what it belongs to or is related to. See page 53 for more on possessive determiners.

Johnson admitted that he regretted **his** decision to leave the company.

> The possessive determiner **his** tells you that it was Johnson's decision.

Demonstrative pronouns are used to identify people or things as being either near or further away.

this   that   these   those

This is Rachel, my friend from school.
Those are my earphones and **that** is my pen!
These are the best brownies you've ever made.

Relative pronouns introduce a clause that gives more information about a noun.

that   which   who   whom   whose

I enjoyed the film **that** we saw last night.
The film, **which** was released in 2013, was a huge box-office success.

The words **when** and **where** are sometimes described as **relative pronouns** when they are used in the same way as the words above.

This is the house **where** I grew up.

! WATCH OUT
In Standard English, do not use **what** instead of **that** in sentences like these:

✔ The film **that** I saw was brilliant.
✘ The film **what** I saw was brilliant.

GRAMMAR

PRONOUNS

Interrogative pronouns are used in questions.

Interrogative pronouns are:

how   what   when   where   who   whom   whose   why

How did you tear your blazer?   **What** is the name of the hotel?
When will Grandma be here?   **Where** did I put my bag?
Who went to the party?   **Whose** are those trainers?
Why haven't you done your homework?
Whom did the Prime Minister choose to fill the position?

Reflexive pronouns

	singular	plural
first person	myself	ourselves
second person	yourself	yourselves
third person	himself, herself or itself	themselves

Reflexive pronouns are used when the object of the verb is the same as the subject of the verb.

They had only two minutes to tidy **themselves** up before going out.
Shut that cupboard door; **you**'ll hurt **yourself** if you hit your head on it.

Reflexive pronouns are also used after a preposition.

James was feeling pleased with **himself** because he had done well in the Science test.

Reflexive pronouns are also used to emphasize that you are referring to a particular person, rather than to anyone else.

Don't bother – I'll do it **myself**.   He **himself** had never been to Scotland.

> **(!) WATCH OUT**
> Some people use the form **themself** when they do not want to specify whether they are referring to men or women, or boys or girls.
>
> Each student is responsible for organizing **themself**.
>
> However, this form is considered by many people to be incorrect in Standard English, so it is best to avoid it. Instead, you can say:
>
> Each student is responsible for organizing **himself** or **herself**.
> or   Students are responsible for organizing **themselves**.

Which pronoun to choose?

In formal writing, use the pronouns ending in **-one**. The pronouns ending in **-body** are less formal.

formal	everyone	someone	anyone	no one
informal	everybody	somebody	anybody	nobody

There is a difference between:

Everyone came.

> This means that all the people came. The word **everyone** is a pronoun.

Every one of the boys came.

> This means that every single boy came. **Every one** is not a pronoun and is usually followed by the word **of**.

Determiners

Determiners are words like **a**, **the**, **some**, **any**, **my**, **each**, **every**, **either** and **no** which are used before a noun, or at the start of a noun phrase. **Determiners** tell you **which one**, **how many** or **how much**.

The girls were in the Y10 netball team.   **Some** people like classical music.
Miss Ahmed sits on **every** committee in the school.
There is **a** bird on the branch.
My pink shoes were ruined!

Articles

The determiners **a/an** and **the** are also called **articles**.

The determiner **a/an** is the **indefinite article**. You use it with a singular noun when the person or thing you are talking about has not yet been mentioned.

A man was approaching.   She had **an** apple in her school bag.

EASY TO REMEMBER
Change **a** to **an** if it comes before a word starting with a vowel sound.

an elephant	and	**an** angry elephant.
a broken egg	but	**an** egg
a box	but	**an** open box
a unit of work	but	**an** easy unit of work
a difficult job	but	**an** extremely difficult job

The determiner **the** is the **definite article**. You use it with a noun:

- when the person or thing you are talking about has already been mentioned

A man was approaching. Aiden felt scared, even though **the** man looked friendly.

- when it is obvious which person or thing you are talking about

She still had some fruit in her school bag. **The** apples were bruised and **the** banana was black.

- when you specify which person or thing you are talking about

The man who was approaching looked friendly.
The fruit in her bag had gone mushy.

- when there is only one particular person or thing

He met **the** King of Spain last year.   **The** sun was shining.

Possessive determiners

Possessive determiners, like possessive pronouns, tell you who something belongs to, or who something relates to.

| my | your | his | her | its | our | their |

Our dog is called Pip.   All of the students had done **their** homework.
It was a terrible shame, in **my** opinion, that the building was demolished.

! There is no apostrophe in **its** when it is being used as a determiner.

Interrogative determiners

The **interrogative determiners** what, which and whose ask which one.

What day are they coming?   **Which** cup is yours?

The determiner **whose** asks who something belongs to, or who something relates to. It is sometimes called an **interrogative possessive determiner**.

Whose bag is this?   **Whose** idea was it to leave the milk out of the fridge?

 There is no apostrophe in **whose**.

Demonstrative determiners

Demonstrative determiners, or **demonstratives**, tell you **which one** by saying whether it is near or far.

Demonstratives are:

this   that   these   those

These decisions made the teacher very unpopular.
Shazia was working on **this** laptop.

GRAMMAR

More determiners

The word **some** is a determiner which is used:

• with a plural noun, or with an uncountable noun, when referring to an unspecified number or amount

Some men were approaching.   She had **some** apples in her school bag.
Would you like **some** sugar in your tea?

• when meaning 'but not everyone' or 'but not everything'

Some students liked the new uniform, but others thought it was horrid.

Determiner or pronoun?

Many words can be used as a determiner or as a pronoun.

Determiners come before a noun.   **Pronouns** are used instead of a noun.

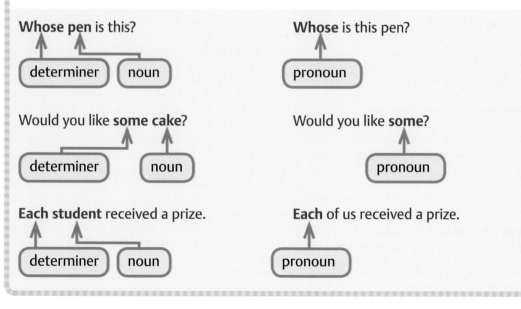

Whose **pen** is this?   **Whose** is this pen?
determiner noun   pronoun

Would you like **some cake**?   Would you like **some**?
determiner noun   pronoun

Each student received a prize.   **Each** of us received a prize.
determiner noun   pronoun

Prepositions

A **preposition** is used before a noun, pronoun or noun phrase and may link it to:

- a verb   I **thought of** you today
- a noun   the **manager of** the library
- an adjective   He was very **fond of** his dog.

The most common preposition is **of**, which has many different uses.

the owner **of** the cafe   the opposite **of** big
the leader **of** the choir   the defeat **of** the enemy
the success **of** our team   the size **of** his feet

Other prepositions often tell you about:

- position or direction

aboard	above	across	against	along	alongside	amid
around	at	beneath	beside	between	beyond	by
from	in	inside	into	near	on	off
on to	opposite	outside	past	round	through	throughout
to	towards	under	upon	via	within	underneath

Her score was **above** the pass mark.   The laptop was **on** the desk.
She looked **through** the window.   The little boy ran **towards** his mother.

- timing

about	after	around	at	before	between
by	during	following	for	from	in
over	pending	per	since	through	throughout
towards	till	to	until	within	

I'll meet you **at** ten o'clock.
Aurelie fell asleep **before** dinner.
Towards the end of the lesson, the fire bell rang.
The band had been successful **throughout** the 2000s.
I normally drink three cups of tea **per** day.

- a link or relationship

about	above	according to	against	by
concerning	despite	except for	from	in
in spite of	less	like	minus	notwithstanding
of	off	on	plus	regarding
save	through	unlike	versus	over
vis-à-vis	without	upon	with	

According to her brother, Aurelie was ill.
It's **against** the law to do that.
Through a combination of hard work and luck, she was successful.

Preposition or adverb?

Some words can be either prepositions or adverbs, depending on how they are used.

We could hear giggling **outside** the classroom.

The word **outside** is a preposition as it is used before the noun phrase, **the classroom**.

We ran **outside**.

Here, the word **outside** is an adverb as it is not followed by a noun, pronoun or noun phrase.

Conjunctions

A **conjunction** links clauses. Some can also link words or phrases. Conjunctions may also be known as connectives. They act as a cohesive device.

Coordinating conjunctions

A **coordinating conjunction** joins clauses, and other phrases or words that are of the same importance in the sentence.

Coordinating conjunctions include:

and	but	or	nor	yet

Mr Smith saw Lucy using a phone; he thought she was a student, **and** tried to confiscate it!

> The conjunction **and** joins the clause **he thought she was a student** to the clause **(he) tried to confiscate it!**

"Mum, please can I borrow your brown shoes **and** bag?" yelled Lizzie.

> The conjunction **and** joins the noun **shoes** to the noun **bag**.

Would you like tea **or** coffee?   He was strict, **but** completely fair.
She did not pass comment, **nor** did she take sides.
He was a tall man, **yet** still graceful.

Subordinating conjunctions

A **subordinating conjunction** introduces a subordinate clause. A **subordinate clause** is not as important as the main clause.

Subordinating conjunctions include:

after	although	as	because	before	for	if
since	so	unless	when	whereas	whether	whilst
though	till	until				

Mr Smith tried to confiscate Lucy's phone **because** he thought she was a student!

The conjunction **because** joins **he thought she was a student** to **Mr Smith tried to confiscate Lucy's phone**.

This is the subordinate, or less important, clause.

"Mum, please can I borrow your brown shoes, **because** I've lost mine?" yelled Lizzie.

The conjunction **because** joins **I've lost mine** to **can I borrow your brown shoes?**

! All the subordinating conjunctions apart from **for** and **so** can be used at the beginning of a sentence, with the subordinate clause fronted (coming first). This makes the information in the subordinate clause seem more important.

Because he thought she was a student, he tried to confiscate her phone!
As I've tidied my room, can I have a friend round?

The subordinating conjunctions **if**, **although** and **though** are also used to introduce a clause which has been reduced to a single word.

If late, students must sign in at student reception.
Although lazy, he was bright.

Conjunctions, adverbs and adverbials: cohesive devices

Conjunctions, as well as many **adverbs and adverbials,** help to show how a piece of text fits together.

The following words are sometimes called connectives. They can connect:

similar ideas	and in other words	moreover furthermore	in addition
contrasting ideas	but in contrast	although nevertheless	however on the other hand
time	finally until	later when	then
causes and results	because therefore	so	as a result
conditions	if unless	provided that	so long as

! Many of these are conjunctions, but not all. Some are adverbs and adverbials. This means that the way you use them is not always the same.

The conjunction **and** can be used in multi-clause sentences.

✔ The goods were faulty, **and** I was treated very badly by your staff.

The word **furthermore** is an adverb. It is not correct to use it in exactly the same way as 'and' (even though it has a similar meaning).

✘ The goods were faulty, **furthermore** I was treated very badly by your staff.

Use **furthermore** at the start of a sentence, or between parenthetic commas.

✔ The goods were faulty. **Furthermore,** I was treated very badly by your staff.

✔ The goods were faulty; **furthermore,** I was treated very badly by your staff.

✔ The goods were faulty; I was, **furthermore,** treated very badly by your staff.

In addition is an adverbial, not a conjunction. In the examples above, it would replace **furthermore**, not **and**.

Phrases

A **phrase** is a group of words that can be understood as a unit.

Noun phrase

A **noun phrase** is a group of words that has a noun as its head, or key word.

The **teacher over there** is **my form tutor**.

> The word **teacher** is a noun. The words **the teacher over there** are a noun phrase.

> The word **tutor** is a noun. The words **my form tutor** are a noun phrase.

Adjective phrase

An **adjective phrase** is a group of words that has an adjective as its head.

She is a **very good** teacher.

> The word **good** is an adjective. The words **very good** are an adjective phrase.

Some of the girls in Year 10 are **really keen** on dance.

> The word **keen** is an adjective. The words **really keen** are an adjective phrase.

Some of the girls in Year 10 are **as keen as anything**.

> The word **keen** is an adjective. The words **as keen as anything** are an adjective phrase.

A phrase whose head is a verb is called a **clause**. See Page 63 for more on clauses.

Adverb phrase

An **adverb phrase** is a group of words that has an adverb as its head.

The teacher removed the spider **as quickly as possible**.

> The word **quickly** is an adverb.
> The words **as quickly as possible** are an adverb phrase.

She was old, and walked **very slowly**.

> The word **slowly** is the adverb that tells you how she walked.
> The words **very slowly** are an adverb phrase.

Preposition phrase

A **preposition phrase** is a group of words that has a preposition as its head.

The mouse ran **along the windowsill**.

> The word **along** is the preposition.
> The words **along the windowsill** are a preposition phrase.

Clauses

A **clause** is a phrase whose head is a verb. It makes that verb more precise.

He **laughed** all the way home.

The word **laughed** is the head in this clause.

A clause answers questions such as **What happened?** (e.g. It rained.) or **How are you feeling?** (e.g. I'm scared.)

A **main clause** is a clause that can be used on its own as a sentence.

The three teachers ran across the playground.

A **subordinate clause** helps to give more meaning to the main clause. It cannot be used on its own as a complete sentence. A subordinate clause often starts with a conjunction such as **because**, **if** or **when**.

The three teachers ran across the playground **because they could see the injured boy**.

conjunction

subordinate clause

A subordinate clause may have a participle or an infinitive as its head.

Seeing the injured boy, the three teachers ran across the playground to help him.

participle

subordinate clause

A subordinate clause cannot exist on its own, as it is not a complete sentence. It needs to go with a main clause.

✗ Because they could see the injured boy.
✔ The teachers ran across the playground, **because they could see the injured boy**.

✗ Seeing the injured boy.
✔ **Seeing the injured boy**, the teachers ran across the playground.

Relative clauses

A **relative clause** is a type of subordinate clause and is introduced using the relative pronouns:

that   which   who   whom   whose

There are two types of relative clause, **defining relative clauses** and **non-defining relative clauses**.

Defining relative clauses specify **which** person or thing you are talking about.

The book **that we bought today** is very interesting.   defining relative clause

This **defining relative clause** tells you **which book** is interesting.

 You do not use commas to separate the defining relative clause from the rest of the sentence.

 The book **that we bought today** is very interesting.
✗ The book, **that we bought today**, is very interesting.

Be careful! In the following sentence, you can omit the relative pronoun **that**.

✔ The book **that we bought today** is very interesting.
✔ The book **we bought today** is very interesting.

We bought the book. Here **the book** is the **object** of the verb **bought**.

In this sentence, you cannot omit the relative pronoun **that**.

 The book **that arrived** today is very interesting.
✗ The book **arrived** today is very interesting.

The book arrived today. Here **the book** is the **subject** of the verb **arrived**.

You cannot omit the relative pronoun if it is the subject of the verb in the relative clause.

Non-defining relative clauses do not specify which person or thing you are talking about.

This book, **which he wrote last year**, is said to be the author's best work.

non-defining relative clause

This non-defining relative clause does not tell you *which* book is interesting. It just tells you when the author wrote it. It only adds some extra information about the book.

 WATCH OUT
Use **parenthetic commas** to separate the non-defining relative clause from the rest of the sentence.

 This book, **which he wrote when he was only 21**, is very interesting.
✔ People were very interested in this book, **which he wrote when he was only 21**.

In formal English, use the relative pronoun **which** rather than **that** in non-defining relative clauses.

✔ The book, **which** he wrote when he was only 21, is very interesting.
✘ The book, **that** he wrote when he was only 21, is very interesting.

Sentences

The form of the main clause in a **sentence** shows whether it is being used as:

- a **statement**

The students wrote their answers on their whiteboards.
This is probably not a good idea.

- a **question**

Have you written your answers on your whiteboards?
Could you give me a hand?

- a **command**
  A command or instruction is usually written in the imperative and
  the verb is the first word in the sentence. The subject is understood as 'you'.

Write your answers on your whiteboards.   **Come in!**

You should do this.   You should do this.

- an **exclamation**
  Exclamations do not always have a subject and verb, and may be a single word.

What a good answer!   Good!

Subject

The **subject** of a verb is often who or what does something (the do-er or be-er). In a statement, the subject is usually the noun, noun phrase or pronoun before the verb.

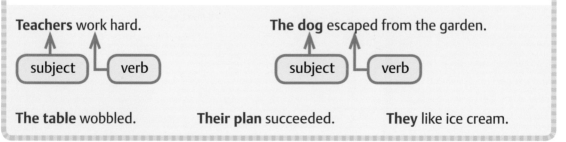

Teachers work hard.   **The dog** escaped from the garden.

subject   verb   subject   verb

The table wobbled.   **Their plan** succeeded.   **They** like ice cream.

The subject can be in the **first**, **second** or **third person**, and can be **singular** (only one) or **plural** (more than one).

The term **person** does not only mean people in this context. Use the chart below to check your understanding.

	singular	plural
	the speaker or writer	several speakers or writers together or the group that includes the speaker or writer
first person:	**I** **I play** football.	**we** **We play** football.
	the person (or thing) being spoken to or written to	the people (or things) being spoken to or written to
second person:	**you** **You play** football.	**you** **You play** football.
	the person or thing being spoken about or written about	the people or things being spoken about or written about
third person:	**he, she, it** **Jack plays** football. **He plays** football. **Nina plays** football. **She plays** football. **The dog plays** with that ball. **It plays** with that ball. **The table was** broken. **London is** a huge city. **Happiness is** not found in money.	**they** **Jack and Nina play** football. **They play** football. **The dogs play** with that ball. **They play** with that ball. **The tables were** broken. **London and Frankfurt are** huge cities. **Happiness and joy are** not found in money.

GRAMMAR

It is important to check that the **subject** and **verb agree**.

This means that if the subject is **third person singular**, the verb form must be **third person singular**.

He plays football.

> **He** is the subject and is singular. **Plays** is the verb and is in the third person singular form, which agrees with **he**.

The match was fantastic.

> **The match** is the subject and is singular. **Was** is the past tense of the verb and is in the third person singular form, which agrees with **the match**.

If the subject is **plural**, the verb form must be **plural**.

They play football.

> **They** is the subject and is plural. **Play** is the verb and is in the third person plural form, which agrees with **they**.

Both matches were fantastic.

> **Both matches** is the subject and is plural. **Were** is the verb and is in the third person plural form, which agrees with **both matches**.

> **Was** or **were**? Use **was** with the first person singular (I) as well as with third person singular subjects.

More examples:

✔ The first **question was** very difficult.
✘ The first **question were** very difficult.

✔ I **was** late for **the exam**!
✘ I **were** late for the exam!

✘ **These opinions**, although not shared by everyone, **is** widely accepted.
✔ **These opinions**, although not shared by everyone, **are** widely accepted.

Object

In some sentences, the verb has an **object**. Normally the **object** is the noun, noun phrase or pronoun which comes just after the verb.

The object is often the person or thing on the receiving end of the action.

Sam was reading **that book**.   object

What was Sam reading? **That book**.

The banks lend **billions** every year.   object

What do the banks lend? **Billions**.

Complement

The verb **be** (and its inflections **am**, **was**, **were**, etc.) is not followed by an object, but is usually followed by a **complement**. There are other verbs which take a complement such as **seem**, **become** and **feel**. The complement is usually an adjective or adjective phrase, or a noun or noun phrase.

The complement can often be found by asking **What is..?**, **What sort of... is ...?** or **What is...like?**

Birmingham is **a city**.   Birmingham is **a huge city**.
                    complement

Birmingham is **huge**.   complement

Object or complement?

In a sentence, if the verb has an object, it is often possible to change it to a passive verb. (See page 39 for more on passives.)

✔ He **felt the earthquake** 50 kilometres away.
✔ **The earthquake was felt** 50 kilometres away.

It is not possible to do this if the verb has a **complement**.

✔ He became **a better teacher.**
✘ A better teacher was become by him.

Transitive or intransitive verbs

Verbs that have an object are **transitive** verbs. Verbs that do not have an object are **intransitive** verbs.

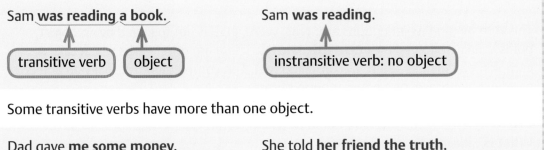

Sam **was reading a book.**
- transitive verb
- object

Sam **was reading.**
- instransitive verb: no object

Some transitive verbs have more than one object.

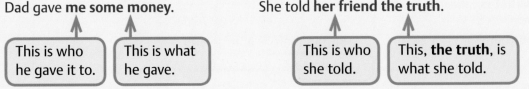

Dad gave **me some money.**
- This is who he gave it to.
- This is what he gave.

She told **her friend the truth.**
- This is who she told.
- This, **the truth**, is what she told.

Types of sentences

A sentence may consist of a main clause on its own. Sentences like this are called **single-clause sentences**. They may also be known as simple sentences.

She knew the truth.

A sentence may also consist of two or more clauses. Sentences like this are called multi-clause sentences. There are different types of multi-clause sentences.

Clauses inside a multi-clause sentence may be **co-ordinated** by means of co-ordinating conjunctions such as **or, and** or **but**. When this happens, the multi-clause sentence may be known as a **compound sentence**.

She knew the truth, and told me.

 Be careful! When the subject of the second clause is the same as the first, it is often omitted.

She knew the truth, **and told me**.

The second clause has the same subject as the first and **she** has been omitted.

Alternatively, one clause may be **subordinate** to another. When this happens, the multi-clause sentence may be known as a complex sentence.

She knew the truth **because she had spoken to the head teacher**.

subordinate clause

Some multi-clause sentences contain both co-ordinate and subordinate patterns.

Having spoken with the head teacher, she knew the truth, and told me.

subordinate clause

Narrative voice

Narrative voice is used to talk about whether a writer chooses to use first person (**I, we**), second person (**you**) or third person (**he/she/it/they**) to present the events and information in a particular text.

First person (I, we)

In a **non-fiction text**, using the first person suggests that the writer has experienced what they are writing about and understands it. This can have the effect of making the reader trust the writer; the reader believes that the writer knows what he or she is talking about.

I saw brightly coloured birds swooping from the upper branches, making loud noises as they flew.

In a **fiction text**, using a first person narrator can make the story feel very real and exciting, as if the reader is experiencing events along with the narrator.

I can't believe I got detention today. It's so unfair!

 Be careful – a first person narrator only allows readers to see one side of the story!

Second person (you)

In a **non-fiction text**, using the second person can make a piece of writing feel very personal, as if the writer is speaking directly to the reader, and as if what is being said applies to or affects the reader.

If you look around you, you will see patterns everywhere in the natural world.

In a **fiction text**, using the second person can make the reader feel as if the narrator is speaking to him or her directly and as if the reader is involved in the action.

You won't believe what happened next. It was hilarious!

> **WATCH OUT**
> Some texts contain a mixture of first and second person. For example, in texts such as speeches and adverts, a mixture of **I**, **you** and **we** can make the reader feel as if he or she is working as a team with the writer or speaker.

Third person (he, she, it, they)

In a **non-fiction text**, using the third person can make a piece of writing feel as if it is unbiased and professional.

She has created a believable character that it is easy to identify with.

In a **fiction text**, using a third person narrator allows the reader to see lots of events from lots of different points of view. It does not limit the story to just what one character sees, does, or thinks.

They knew that winter was coming, and that it was time for them to be gone.

> **WATCH OUT**
> Some texts contain a mixture of third and second person. For example, in an advice text it is a good idea to avoid using the first person, as it can make readers feel as if what you are saying does not apply to them. It can be more effective to make general statements using the third person so that readers will feel as if they are not the only person to experience a particular difficulty. Combining this with the second person to address readers can make them feel as if you are addressing them and their problems directly.
>
> It is a large school but you are given a map to help you find your way around.

> **WATCH OUT**
> In formal writing, for example in English Literature essays or when you are writing accounts of experiments in Science, you can use the third person. This will make your writing seem professional and unbiased.

Effective writing

Vary sentence types in your writing

By using a variety of sentence types you will create text that is enjoyable, rather than repetitive and boring. If your audience likes reading what you have written, your message is likely to be understood easily: this is effective communication.

Think about sentences and their punctuation

A common mistake is to run sentences together without punctuation, or to use the wrong punctuation.

✘   Kate laughed the book she was reading was really funny.

This should be two sentences.

✔   Kate laughed. The book she was reading was really funny.

    Remember to use a full stop between two sentences, not a comma. If the sentences are closely linked, you can use a semicolon.

✔   Kate laughed. The book she was reading was really funny.
✔   Kate laughed; the book she was reading was really funny.

Be careful with tenses

In this example, different tenses are used correctly.

✔   I **went** to see my friend yesterday, and I **will go** again tomorrow.

The past tense **went** matches **yesterday**.   The future **will go** matches **tomorrow**.

In the example below, the tense changes in a way that is not correct.

✘   He **shows** that war is senseless: that ordinary people are fighting and dying.
He **showed** it by...

GRAMMAR

Be careful with 'there is' and 'there are'

Use **there is** before a singular or uncountable noun, pronoun or noun phrase.

✔ **There is** still one **question** left to do.
✔ **There is** still **work** to do.

Use **there are** before a plural noun.

✔ **There are** still two **questions** left to do.
✔ **There are** loads of **cakes** left.

In everyday spoken English, many people use **there's** with a plural noun. This is not appropriate in formal writing.

✔ **There are** two **reasons** for this.
✘ **There's** two **reasons** for this.
✘ **There is** two **reasons** for this.

'My friend and I' or 'my friend and me'?

Check if you should use **and I** or **and me** with this simple trick.

Using written Standard English, your sentence should still make sense if you take out the **other person's name** and the word **and**.

✘ **Sally and me** walked to Selma's house.
✘ **Me** walked to Selma's house.

✔ **Sally and I** walked to Selma's house.
✔ **I** walked to Selma's house.

✘ Anita came with **Sally and I** to Selma's house.
✘ Anita came with **I** to Selma's house.

✔ Anita came with **Sally and me** to Selma's house.
✔ Anita came with **me** to Selma's house.

Standard and non-standard English

Standard English is the English taught in schools. It is used in most books, newspapers and formal documents. It is also used in communications such as the news on the television, radio or Internet. Most of your written work needs to be in Standard English.

It can be spoken using different accents, e.g. a West Midlands accent or a Welsh accent.

Non-standard English is English that may be different in different parts of the country. It is mostly used in speech, especially in informal situations. It can be used when writing down what people have said.

"It **ain't** my fault!"   "You would have fallen if I **hadn't've** saved you."

In **non-standard English**, spelling, punctuation and grammar may be different from Standard English.

Verb forms, subject-verb agreement, pronouns, determiners, prepositions, adverbs and negatives may all be different from Standard English.

We was lucky to get away with it!   Standard English is **We were**.

He **didn't** play with **nobody**.   double negative

A double negative uses two or more negative words in one phrase or sentence. Double negatives should be avoided in Standard English.

✗   We **didn't** see **nothing**.   double negative

✔   We saw **nothing**.
✔   We **didn't** see anything.

GRAMMAR

Most of the following text is written in Standard English, using standard spellings, punctuation and grammar.

In the extract, Mr Smith uses Standard English, but his speech is not formal as he uses contractions such as **can't** and **you've**.

Millie uses non-standard English, as well as informal expressions such as **and all** and **for a bit**. Where she uses non-standard English, the Standard English equivalent is shown alongside.

	Standard English
"Millie," said Mr Smith, "I can't see your name on this list. Did you do your online Maths?"	
"Yes, Sir! I done it!" declared Millie, looking aggrieved.	I did it
"Right," said Mr Smith. "You've done it, have you? Let's have another look, then... No, your name's still not here. When did you do it?"	I did it
"I done it last night, Sir! An' I saved it, an' all!"	and
"That's good, Millie. What time was this?" Mr Smith was still staring at his laptop screen, but then he looked up and asked again, "What time was this, Millie?"	I did it
"Well," said Millie, thinking for a moment, "I done it around 9 o'clock... It was about then... I told me mum I was gonna watch tv and do it after. Yeah, it were about nine.	my mum / going to / Yes, it was / afterwards
"Are you sure you saved your work, Millie?" asked Mr Smith mildly.	
"Yes, Sir. I finished it just when Mum said I were to go to bed, and just then I seen me friend walking past so I called her and she come in for a bit. So I turned off the computer and... oh! No, Sir, I didn't save me work..."	I was / I saw my friend / she came / my work

77

Formal and informal language

When deciding whether to use formal or informal language, it is important to think about your audience.

very formal	fairly formal	fairly informal	very informal
letter to your head teacher	most school work	letter to your mother's friend	text or email to your friend
exams		note-taking	
official letters and emails			shopping list

Formal language is the language used in official or formal situations. In most of the writing that you do in school, you need to use formal language. Exceptions include note-taking and when you are told to write informally.

When writing formally use:

- Standard English
- the correct conventions when you start and end a letter to someone
- formal vocabulary that you may not use in everyday conversation
- abstract nouns, rather than verbs, to express ideas
- the passive voice rather than the active voice

When writing formally, do not use contractions, colloquialisms or question tags. Do not use random capital letters.

passive

It is anticipated that all groups will participate. Indeed, full participation is required.

more formal than **expected**

more formal than **take part**

more formal than **Actually**

Full participation is required is more formal than **Everyone must take part.**

Formal job application letter

Draft letter

~~Hi Victor~~ Dear Mr Frankenstein,

~~I'd~~ I would like to apply for the job of ~~lab~~ laboratory assistant ~~saw it in the paper~~ which was advertised in the newspaper. ~~I've got tons~~ I have a great deal of experience in this ~~kinda thing~~ type of work. ~~I'd love to work at your place.~~ I would be delighted to take up a position with you. ~~See my cv.~~ Please see the enclosed cv. ~~Should be fun!~~ I look forward to working with you. ~~Cheers~~ Yours sincerely,

Fritz Klein

In a formal letter, you either start with: **Dear** + the person's title and surname or **Dear Sir/Madam,**
Contractions are only used in informal writing.
The word **lab** is an informal word for **laboratory**.
The word **tons** is an informal word that means 'a lot'.
This is not polite enough for a formal letter.
Exclamation marks are not often used in formal writing.
To finish a formal letter use: • **Yours sincerely,** if the letter starts with **Dear** + the person's name • **Yours faithfully,** if the letter starts with **Dear Sir/Madam,**

Final letter

Dear Mr Frankenstein,

I would like to apply for the job of laboratory assistant which was advertised in the newspaper. I have a great deal of experience in this type of work. I would be delighted to take up a position with you.

Please see the enclosed CV.

I look forward to working with you.

Yours sincerely,
Fritz Klein

GRAMMAR

Informal language is the language we use in everyday situations.

In writing, informal language is used for:

- letters and emails to family and friends
- text messages
- notes
- shopping lists and to-do lists

Informal language used in writing is likely to include:

- random capital letters for emphasis
- lots of exclamation marks for emphasis
- contractions
- colloquialisms
- question tags

A **colloquialism** is a word or phrase that is used mainly in everyday conversation.

Homework is **a pain**!
Miss Shafi took **the kids** on a trip to London.

A **question tag** is a short question 'tagged' on to the end of a sentence. Question tags are used when you are asking someone to respond to what you have said.

He's a teacher, **isn't he?**

auxiliary verb   pronoun

Informal email

Hey you!

How's it going? It's been such a SCORCHER today, hasn't it? I'm having a great time! Bring your cozzie and we'll head for the beach.

Byeeee

Jane

The **contraction** 'how's' (joining two words **how** and **is**) is used.

How's it going? is more formally written as **How are you?**

This is a **colloquialism** meaning that it is very hot.

Capital letters emphasize how hot it is.

question tag

The word **cozzie** is an informal word for swimming costume.

To **head for** means 'to go to'.

Repetition of the letter **e** mimics how the word might be said in speech.

FORMAL AND INFORMAL LANGUAGE

81

Contractions

When a word is made shorter by dropping one or more letters, this is called a **contraction**, or **short form**. **Contractions** are used a great deal when writing direct speech, and also in informal writing.

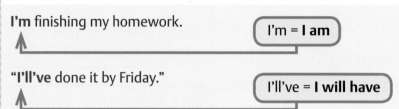

I'm finishing my homework.

I'm = **I am**

"**I'll've** done it by Friday."

I'll've = **I will have**

Contractions are written as a single word.

I **don't** think I can come, sorry.

Contractions use an apostrophe to show where letters have been omitted:

short form	long form
I'm	I am
don't	do not
can't	cannot
what's	what is

The following contractions also involve other changes:

shan't = shall not   **won't** = will not

Contractions that end in **-a** do not have an apostrophe. These contractions are not Standard English.

kinda = kind of   **gonna** = going to

In most formal writing, including most school work, the correct style is to use long forms, rather than contractions.

Dear Sir/Madam,
I would like to apply... (not: **I'd** like to apply...)

Some **contractions** may be appropriate if you are deliberately adopting a **conversational tone**.

Perhaps you**'ve** been wondering what secondary school is like...

Direct speech and reported speech

Direct speech is when you write the exact words that someone says. It is shown by using speech marks. Speech marks are also called **inverted commas**.

"I've made you a sandwich," said Mum. "It's your favourite — chicken with lettuce and cucumber."

"Thanks!" called Daz, as he dodged past her, "but I'll go to the canteen today. Everyone else goes there."

"But it's so expensive."

"I've got some money. You can have the sandwich! Thanks anyway. See you later... Can Cal come home with me after school?"

"Yes," sighed Mum. "See you later."

"Bye!"

For direct speech:
* put speech marks around the words spoken
* start a new paragraph whenever the speaker changes
* only include the exact words the speaker says inside the speech marks
* put punctuation marks inside the speech marks.
* It is not always necessary to state the name of who is speaking but if there are more than two speakers, it may be clearer to give the name of the person speaking.

Reported speech is when you report what someone says without using the exact words spoken. Reported speech is also called **indirect speech**.

Daz said that he would go to the canteen that day.

For **reported speech**:

- do not use speech marks
- pronouns, tenses and adverbials of time may need to change

direct speech	reported speech
'I'll go to the canteen **today,'** said Daz.	Daz said that **he would go** to the canteen **that day**.
'Can Cal come home with **me** after school?' asked Daz.	Daz asked if Cal **could** come home with **him** after school.

- For reported speech use **whether** or **if** to introduce a yes-no question.

Daz asked **whether** Cal could come home with him after school.

- Do not use a question mark after a reported question.

Daz asked if Cal could come home with him after school.

In reported speech, the word **that** is often used to introduce a statement, especially in formal writing. It can be omitted, especially when speaking or writing less formally.

Daz told his mother **that** he would go to the canteen.
Daz said **he'd** go to the canteen.

 Avoid using **say** too often. Instead, vary your vocabulary by using a word which gives more specific information.

Sam **recounted** the day's events.   Sunil **promised** to help me.
He **explained** what he intended to do.

Choose your words carefully

The aim in writing is to communicate an idea as clearly as possible to the reader.

✔ Sometimes, this means being **concise** or using one word instead of several, or fewer words instead of more.

Instead of writing

The dog was **small** and **rat-like** and looked **as though it liked to fight**.

you could write

The dog was **stunted** and looked **aggressive**.

✔ Sometimes, it can help the reader to imagine more clearly what you are writing about if you use **specific** or **precise** words rather than general words.

For example, **flower** is a general word, but **rose**, **daffodil**, **lily** and **tulip** are more specific, because they refer to types of flowers.

Instead of writing

The garden was full of **flowers**.

you could write

The garden was a mass of **lilies** and **roses**.

✔ Sometimes it can help the reader to imagine more clearly what you are writing about if you use **figurative** or **metaphorical** language:

The lawn was **a carpet of** daisies.

This means that the lawn was covered with daisies, just as a carpet covers a floor.

Using synonyms and antonyms in your writing

Synonyms are words that mean the same or nearly the same as each other, such as **enormous** and **huge**, or **horrid** and **nasty**.

Instead of saying that someone ate a whole pizza, you could write:

He **wolfed down** a whole pizza! or He **polished off** a whole pizza!

Sometimes you can choose between synonyms without altering the meaning. For instance, a building might be **huge**, **immense** or **colossal**. You can choose any of these words and it makes no difference to the meaning.

At other times you may need to think more carefully about which synonym to use. For example, some are more formal than others.

In a piece of school work, you might write:

The cake was **delicious**.

In your diary, a blog or in a message or email to a friend, you might write:

The cake was **yummy**.

Words such as **bad**, **big**, **good** and **nice** can be useful, but you can make your writing more interesting by choosing synonyms which occur less frequently.

Instead of describing someone as **beautiful**, try using the word **radiant**.

Does the phrase **big building** have enough impact? If not, try using a more precise and unusual phrase such as **monstrous edifice** instead.

Before choosing an alternative word, check that it has the right meaning:

a **nice** person   **nice** weather

⬆   ⬆

friendly, kind, thoughtful   pleasant, warm

Use a thesaurus to find useful synonyms and to learn how they can be used.

GRAMMAR

Antonyms are words that mean the opposite of each other.

In the 100m sprint, Jess got off to a **quick** start.
In the 100m sprint, Jess got off to a **slow** start.

Using opposites can be an effective way of showing contrast.

His mother found ripe cheese quite **revolting**; for him, it was the most **delicious** treat imaginable.

Using opposites can also be a good way of linking ideas, while avoiding repetition.

Unfortunately, **he failed** his exam. Even though **he had not passed**, the college accepted him, and...

Remember that you can change the meaning of many words by adding a prefix such as **un-**, **im-** or **dis-** at the start of a word.

I was very **happy** to be going on holiday without my parents.
I was very **unhappy** to be going on holiday without my parents.

The head **agreed** with the students' decision and employed the teacher whom they liked.
The head **disagreed** with the students' decision and employed the teacher whom they **disliked**.

You can also change the meaning of some words by changing the suffix (the ending).

His work is always **careless**: it shows signs of being rushed.
His work is always **careful**: it shows signs of being done with great attention to detail.

See pages 122 and 124 for more on prefixes and suffixes.

Paragraphs and cohesion

When writing a longer piece of text, it is important to fit the text together so that it is easy to read and understand. This text, about the Olympic Games, is annotated with small numbers. Look on the next pages to find the information about these features.

The Olympic Games

The ancient Games

The first Olympic Games took place in Ancient Greece about 776BC. [1] They were held in an area called Olympia. In **these** [5] first Games, there was only one event: a short running race from one end of the stadium to the other. **Later,** [6] more events, such as chariot racing, were added. [2]

Originally, women and girls were not allowed to participate in the Olympic Games. [1] **As a consequence,** [6] a separate **event,** [9] called the Herannic Games after the goddess Hera, was held for women. As in the **Olympic Games,** [10] women **took part** [9] in running races. **They** [4] wore short dresses, called chitons. However, male **competitors** [11] in the Olympic Games wore no clothes at all.

The modern Games

Hundreds of years later, [3] the modern Olympic Games began in the nineteenth century, with the foundation of the International Olympic Committee (IOC). The first modern Games were held in Athens in 1896.

In contrast to [8] the ancient **Olympic Games,** [10] the modern Games (and their competitors) are very varied. Men and women take part (**although** [7] there are only a few instances in which they are in competition with each other) and there are events both for able-bodied contestants and for para-Olympians. The Winter Olympics allow for cold-weather sports such as skiing and snowboarding, and the 2012 summer Olympics in London added new events, including female boxing.

As London 2012 demonstrated, the modern Olympics bring competitors from around the world to participate in a huge variety of events. What would the runners in ancient Olympia, with their single race, make of the modern Games?

GRAMMAR

Paragraphs are groups of sentences which belong together and which are clearly separated on the page from each other.

To show a new paragraph:

* leave a line empty between paragraphs, or
* **indent** the first line of each paragraph. This means leaving some space between the margin and the first word of the paragraph. It is important to leave the same-sized space at all paragraphs.

It does not matter which method you use, as long as you use the same method throughout your piece of writing.

Within a paragraph, the sentences are usually about the same thing. Often, the first sentence (the **topic sentence** [1]) tells the reader what the paragraph is about, and is followed by other sentences which give more details.

Start a new paragraph when you are going to start writing about something different:

* in an article or letter — for a different aspect [2], opinion, idea or example
* in a narrative piece — for a different person, time, location or event
* in direct speech — whenever the speaker changes

The first sentence in the new paragraph often contains one or more links back to previous paragraphs. An example in the extract is **Hundreds of years later,** [3] which links the modern Games to the ancient ones by talking about the amount of time between them.

Headings and subheadings can be used to draw attention to the content of sections of non-fiction writing.

GRAMMAR

PARAGRAPHS AND COHESION

Cohesion refers to the ways in which the writer makes the different parts of a text link together, for example, by:

- grouping sentences together in paragraphs
- using particular words and phrases to link ideas
- linking different paragraphs together

Links across sentences and paragraphs are made by referring to something that has been mentioned already, or to something that is mentioned later. This may involve the use of

- pronouns, such as **they** [4]
- determiners, such as **these** [5]
- adverbials (often fronted adverbials), such as **As a consequence** [6]
- conjunctions, e.g. **although** [7]
- prepositions, or phrases that act as prepositions, such as **In contrast to** [8]
- synonyms, or other words which refer to a similar thing; for example **to take part** [9] means **to participate**, and **event** [9] refers to something that is similar to the **Games**
- repeated words, such as **Olympic Games** [10]
- related words which are in a different word class, such as **competitors** [11] and **compete**.

The words and phrases that link ideas in a text are called **cohesive devices**. Each different cohesive device within a text is part of a reference chain. An example of a reference chain in the Olympic Games text is: the first **Olympic Games** [1] – **they** [4] – **these** [5] **first Games**.

 Punctuation is also a cohesive device; it shows how ideas fit together.

Dinner is usually at 6 p.m.; however, it will be later this evening.

This tells you that the second sentence is closely linked to the first.

Correcting your written work

This extract shows how to mark up a text with corrections neatly. The most important thing is that your corrections can be easily understood by the reader.

Tablets on the table!

The latest idea to arise from school council meeting's is a proposal to spend some

of the recently raised PTA funds on a small number of tablet devices for the

school library. ~~Like this idea?~~ *Do you like this idea?* Then read on for more inf*o*rmation about the

suggested scheme, and ideas of how to get involved in our campaign. ~~Think it's a~~ *Do you think that this is*

terrible idea? Read on anyway, and try to keep an open mind. ~~Maybe~~ *Perhaps* some of

the arguments here will persuade you that this is the best idea to have come

out of a meeting since the sixth form voted to abolish uniform.

Who will be able to use the tablets?

The answer is that anyone ~~will~~, whether a member of staff or a student, will be

able to use the tablets. Staff may claim that they are always too busy, but those

shiny new gadgets may turn out to be as tempting as one of those new paninis

that you can get in the canteen. If you could choose between marking, report

writing or a quick dose of 'Wuthering Heights', which would it be?

How many e-readers will be available?

This depends on how much money we can raise. The initial hope is *to* buy at least

20 dev*c*ies.

Correcting your written work

If you have planned your work carefully and referred to your plan as you write, you are likely to make few errors. However, when you check your work, you may find things that you need to change. This page contains advice about making changes as neatly as possible to handwritten or printed work.

For examples of some of the following points, see the text, *Tablets on the table!*

- Cross out with a single line and make sure that the line is visible.

- Do not scribble.

- Do not write on top of your original writing, unless you are sure that the new letter will be clear. It is much better to cross out neatly and write the correct letter above.

- Use a ∧ or ⋀ to show the new letter and where it should go. Use the same mark each time.

- **Correct your punctuation legibly. For example:**
  - When striking out a comma or apostrophe, make sure that it is clear that it is no longer supposed to be there.

  - Full stops should not look like bullet points! If your full stop is not clear, make it clearer, but do not exaggerate it.

  - If you need to cross out a full stop, make sure that you do not turn it into a comma.

- **Make sure that punctuation marks are in the correct position:**
  - A semicolon (;) is made up of a comma with the full stop just above it, level with the top of letters like a, e, n and o.

  - A colon (:) is made up of a full stop with another full stop just above it, level with the top of letters like a, e, n and o.

  - Use an asterisk (*) to show where additional text should be inserted. Then repeat the asterisk next to your additional text. You normally write this at the bottom of the page.

- If you want to show that you meant to start a new paragraph, use the symbol // to show a paragraph break.

Proofreading and correcting work written on a computer

When writing on a computer, remember the following points:

- Make sure you have switched the preferred language to UK English. This will affect not only the spellchecker, but the grammar checker as well.

- When a change is suggested, make sure that you read it before clicking 'accept'. You may need to scroll down to another suggestion.

- Some words are used much more often than others, and are therefore more likely to be the words that you want. For example, if your spellchecker picks up 'alot' it is more likely that you intended to write ' a lot' (= many), rather than 'allot' (= give).

- If you are not sure if a suggested word or phrase is the right one, look up its meaning.

- If you click on 'ignore all', then the word (or misspelling) will be accepted throughout the document. Similarly, if you click on 'add to dictionary', then the word will continue to be accepted as correct in the future. Take care not to click these by accident.

- Remember that even modern spellcheckers and grammar checkers may miss some mistakes.

- Many words are easy to mix up when you are typing quickly. Examples include **from/form**, **quiet/quite** and **then/them**.

- You can set your word-processing program to correct spellings and capitalization automatically. This can save time and effort, but it can also create bad habits in your handwritten work.

- There are times when automatic capitalization is not helpful, for example if you are keying lists or notes rather than sentences.

Punctuation

Punctuation marks are used in sentences to make the meaning clear. Even a slight change of punctuation can change the meaning of a sentence.

Let's eat Granny!	Let's eat, Granny!
a man-eating tiger	a man eating tiger

Punctuation marks

•

A **full stop** comes at the end of a sentence. It shows that a sentence is complete and finished.

This is a full sentence.	I am the tallest in my class.
I like swimming.	Let's go to the cinema.
We are having lunch now.	You can text me later.

ABC

Capital letters are used at the beginning of sentences.

We're going abroad this summer.

Capital letters are used for days of the week and months of the year.

Monday Tuesday Wednesday Thursday Friday Saturday Sunday

January	February	March	April	May	June
July	August	September	October	November	December

PUNCTUATION

Capital letters are used for **proper nouns**: names of things, people, places and titles.

- people, e.g. *Cheryl Cole, Jack, Sureena*

- brands, e.g. *Ferrari, Apple, Samsung*

- places, e.g. *London, New York, Mumbai*

- books, e.g. *War Horse, The Hunger Games, Lord of the Flies*

- computer games, e.g. *Mario Kart, Minecraft, Gran Turismo*

- plays and musicals, e.g. *Macbeth, War Horse, Wicked!*

- films, e.g. *Skyfall, The Woman in Black, Iron Man 3*

- paintings and sculptures, e.g. *Mona Lisa, Campbell's Soup Cans, The Scream, David, Angel of the North*

Capital letters are used for **abbreviations**.

RSPCA   ICT   BBC

WATCH OUT
Always use a capital letter when you use the personal pronoun **I** to write about yourself, or if you are writing a story with a first person narrator.

I raised £100 for charity!   Silently, I crept down the hallway.

PUNCTUATION

?

A **question mark** is used at the end of a sentence to show that it is a question.

Where are you?   What are you doing at the weekend?

Who was that?   Do you not like football?

How are you?   What time is it?

Are you coming to the cinema with us?

!

An **exclamation mark** is used at the end of a sentence to show that it is an exclamation.

An exclamation mark can be used to show that the sentence is about something urgent or surprising, or to show a strong emotion such as delight or anger.

It's a goal!   What a lovely present!

Fantastic work!   I can't believe you just said that!

Run!   What a good answer!

An **exclamation mark** can be used at the end of a sentence to show that it is a command: a command is a sentence which gives an order or an instruction.

Run!   Sit down!

Have some cake!   Come in!

Put your books away!

PUNCTUATION

,

A **comma** is used to separate items in a list.

I like to eat apples, seeds, grapes and nuts.

Javad wanted to visit Spain, Italy, Greece and Portugal.

Make sure you bring pens, pencils and a notebook.

WATCH OUT
In some texts you may see the **serial comma** (also known as the Oxford comma). This is when a comma is used in a list of three or more items before the last **and** or **or**.

I ate an orange, an apple, and some raspberries.

serial comma

The serial comma is optional and was traditionally used by Oxford University Press. Not everyone uses it, so it is generally better to avoid it in your own work.

A **comma** is often used before a coordinating conjunction such as **or**, **and** or **but** to separate the two clauses in a multi-clause sentence.

I like swimming, but I love ice skating!

first clause   second clause

Do you want an ice cream, or would you prefer a biscuit?

We're just waiting for Cheri, and then we'll set off.

COMMAS

A **comma** is also used after a subordinate clause at the start of a multi-clause sentence.

When he realized how much money I had spent, my dad went mad.

This is the subordinate clause.

Smiling to herself, Jazmin walked out of the room.

After they had finished marking, the teachers had a meeting to discuss the grades.

Commas are also used in sentences if a subordinate clause is inserted into the middle of the main clause.

 Put a **comma** before and after the subordinate clause.

Jon's suggestion, because he was so worried about global warming, was that the whole class should start a cycle-to-school campaign.

subordinate clause

After three weeks, if you have been practising regularly, you should find that your technique has improved.

Caliban was left alone, smiling and laughing to himself, on the deserted island.

The children, wet and weary after their walk, were all given hot tea and biscuits.

For more on using **subordinate clauses** and **main clauses**, see page 63.

PUNCTUATION

A **comma** can be used after an adverb or an adverbial if you are using it at the start of a sentence.

Luckily, I had revised all the topics that came up in the exam. [adverb]

Surprisingly, only seven pupils signed up for the trip. [adverb]

To his horror, he saw the ball hit the back of the net. [adverbial]

With a shake, the dog dried itself off. [adverbial]

If you are addressing a person or group of people directly, you use **commas** to separate their name from the rest of the sentence.

Tell me, kids, what film do you want to watch?

Nita, we're going to be late!

Let's eat, Grandma.

COLONS

A **colon** can be used to introduce a list.

I play the following sports: hockey, badminton, tennis and rounders.

There are three friends in the book: Harry, Ron and Hermione.

We are going to need: knives, forks, spoons and glasses.

They come in four colours: red, blue, yellow and green.

A **colon** can be used to introduce examples or explanations. The examples or explanations, which give you more information, come after the colon.

Athletes need to eat lots of high-protein snacks: eggs, fish and steak are popular choices.

I like the colour blue: it is the colour of my favourite team.

The house has all the modern luxuries you could wish for: there are six bedrooms, all with their own bathrooms, a gym and a home cinema.

Swans have large webbed feet: they use them to propel themselves through water more efficiently.

! WATCH OUT
Do not use a capital letter for the word that comes after a colon, unless it is a proper noun. Proper nouns are the names of people, places, things or titles.

✔ Something moved at the bottom of the garden: **it** was just our dog.

✘ Something moved at the bottom of the garden: **It** was just our dog.

PUNCTUATION

;

A **semicolon** can be used to separate two sentences or main clauses which are of equal importance.

The film was brilliant; I had a great time.

The room is hot; there are a lot of people dancing.

WATCH OUT

Sometimes you may see commas used to join sentences that are strongly connected. This is considered to be incorrect. If you want to join sentences, use a semicolon or a colon.

✔ Staff soon discovered the damage; the teacher was furious.

> The semicolon here is correct because it joins two main clauses which could stand alone as full sentences.

A **semicolon** can be used in lists. Semicolons are used to separate longer phrases in a list.

The children need to bring with them: a hot-water bottle or an extra blanket if the weather is cold; a cup, a plate and a bowl; a knife, a fork and a spoon.

I need: yoghurt; as many bananas as you have; a tub of vanilla ice cream; and chocolate to sprinkle on top.

We all brought four things: a pair of trainers; a brightly coloured shirt; a swimming costume; and some kind of musical instrument.

—

A **dash** is sometimes used in informal writing in the same way that commas and semicolons are used: to show where clauses begin or end; to indicate that two sentences are linked to each other; or to introduce items in a list.

! Avoid using dashes in this way in formal writing.

informal   Jogging takes it out of you — especially if you aren't used to it.

formal   Jogging takes it out of you, especially if you aren't used to it.

informal   There was a pool, a cinema and free use of the pedaloes on the beach — it was the best holiday ever!

formal   There was a pool, a cinema and free use of the pedaloes on the beach; it was the best holiday ever!

( ) , —

Brackets, **commas** or **dashes** can all be used to separate a word or phrase that has been added to a sentence as an explanation or afterthought.

The word or phrase inside the brackets, commas or dashes is called a **parenthesis** or is said to be **in parenthesis**.

Commas used this way are sometimes called **parenthetic commas**.

If you take out the word or phrase between the two brackets, commas or dashes, the sentence should still makes sense on its own.

I looked up (squinting because of the sun) and saw the birds flying.

I looked up, squinting because of the sun, and saw the birds flying.

I looked up — squinting because of the sun — and saw the birds flying.

PUNCTUATION

•••

An **ellipsis** is a set of three dots used to show that a word has been missed out or a sentence is not finished.

Suddenly, the door opened...   Don't tell me...

An **ellipsis** is used to show that words have been missed out of a long quote. This is a useful technique in essays as it can save you time.

From the lines, "I picked him up... with just a toothbrush and the good earth for a bed", we learn that the hitchhiker is a drifter and not tied to a routine like the narrator.

—

A **hyphen** is used to join two or more words, or to join some prefixes to words.

! A **hyphen** is shorter than a **dash** and does not have space on either side of it.

co-ordinate   co-own   great-aunt   fair-haired   sky-blue
a mix-up   a 15-year-old boy   a bad-tempered teacher

Hyphens are very important for making meaning clear.

a man eating tiger   a man-eating tiger

↑   ↑

This could be a man eating a tiger.   The hyphen shows it is a tiger that eats men.

PUNCTUATION

Speech marks, or **inverted commas**, are used in writing direct speech. Direct speech is the exact words that someone has said.

"I'm beginning to understand," he said.
"Finally!" she replied.
"We're too late," I said.
"Can we meet up tomorrow?" Sarah asked.

WATCH OUT
The punctuation at the end of the words that are spoken always comes **inside** the final set of speech marks.

✔ "Can I talk to you please?" she whispered.
✘ "Can I talk to you please"? she whispered.

Inverted commas, or quotation marks, are used in writing to show that you are quoting what someone has written or said.

Candy describes The Boss as 'a pretty nice fella'.

Duffy uses the words 'puce', 'yellow', 'green' and 'red' to make the reader think of the colours they might see in a bruise.

EASY TO REMEMBER
You may see single (' ') or double (" ") speech marks when you are reading. Both of these are correct, and, unless you are given specific instructions, it is not important which style you use in your own writing. However, whichever you choose, you must use it consistently through your work.

'I'll bring chocolate and popcorn,' Kate said.
"Where are you?" I whispered nervously.

PUNCTUATION

,

An **apostrophe** is used to show that letters are missed out of a word, for example in **won't** or **can't**. Words like this are called **contractions**.

I am sure I **didn't** pick up the pen.

> The two words **did** and **not** are joined and the apostrophe replaces the letter **o** in **not**.

I **won't** eat all the biscuits, I promise!

> Here, the two words **will** and **not** are joined. The apostrophe replaces more than one letter.

it + is / has = it's
who + is / has = who's
he + is / has = he's
she + is / has = she's
we + are = we're
you + are = you're
he + had = he'd
she + would = she'd
had + not = hadn't

do + not = don't
can + not = can't
does + not = doesn't
should + not = shouldn't
would + have = would've
could + not = couldn't
could + have = could've
shall + not = shan't
will + not = won't

!

WATCH OUT
It is easy to confuse **its** and **it's**.

There is no apostrophe in the word **its** when it is being used as a determiner.

The peregrine had two eggs in **its** nest.

> The word **its** is a possessive determiner like **his** or **her**.

105

An **apostrophe** is also used to show ownership or possession. This means that something belongs to someone or something, or is intended to be used by them.

- If a singular word does not end in **-s**, add **'s** :

  the boy's pen   the dog's bowl

- If a singular word ends in **-s**, add either **'s** or just **'** :

  James's hat   Nicholas' hat

- If a singular word ends in **-ss**, still add **'s** :

  the princess's crown   the boss's chair
  the witness's statement

- If a plural ends in **-s**, just add **'** :

  the girls' changing room   the visitors' car park
  the calves' horns

- If a plural doesn't end in **-s**, add **'s** :

  children's books   men's coats
  women's shoes   the people's parliament

> **!** **WATCH OUT**
> Do not use an apostrophe to make a word plural!
>
> ✔ Cauliflowers are half price!
> ✗ Cauliflower's are half price!

PUNCTUATION

- **Bullet points** are used to draw attention to important information within a document so that it is easy to identify key facts and issues. Here are some guidelines on how to use bullet points.

- The text introducing the list of bullet points should end with a colon.

- If the text that follows the bullet point is not a proper sentence, it does not need to start with a capital letter and end with a full stop.

Plan for the holidays:
- finish book
- mend bike
- tidy room

- If the text that follows the bullet point is a complete sentence, it should begin with a capital letter and end with a full stop.

Students gave the following reasons for choosing to join after-school clubs:
- It gives them a chance to learn new skills.
- They enjoy spending more time with their friends.
- It allows them to get to know their teachers.

Bullet points are a good way of making a text look clear and attractive. They are very useful in advice texts or instructions where readers will want to be able to find information quickly. However, you should avoid using too many bullet-pointed sections in the same piece of writing as this could become confusing.

WATCH OUT
Avoid using bullet points in formal essays or fiction texts.

underlining

Underlining can be used to help to structure a piece of text, along with headings, bullet points or, on the computer, emboldening words. When you are writing a piece of text which has a number of elements, decide on your structural devices and use them consistently throughout the text.

✔ <u>The Olympic Games</u>
The ancient games
The modern games

✘ <u>THE OLYMPIC GAMES</u>
<u>The ancient games</u>
<u>The modern games</u>

/

A **/** or **forward slash** is often used instead of the word 'or' when offering alternatives. It is generally used with no space on either side of it. It is also used in computing to separate elements of web addresses.

Dear Sir/Madam,   www.oxforddictionaries.com/childrens

&

The symbol **&** is called an **ampersand**. It is used instead of the word 'and' in combinations such as **Smith & Co.**

*

The symbol ***** is called an **asterisk**. A superscript* asterisk is placed next to a word. It points the reader to a footnote at the bottom of the page where there will be more information relating to that part of the text. Asterisks can also be used to indicate missing letters and have a number of different uses online as well.

* 'Superscript' means written smaller and higher than the rest of the text.

Spelling

Spelling can be tricky because English words are not always written the way that they sound. Some words are difficult to spell because they have unusual letter combinations or seem inconsistent; some words are easily confused; some words change their spelling according to how they are used; and sometimes different rules apply to words for no apparent reason. All this has come about because the English language is made up of words from a wide range of different influences over thousands of years. It is constantly changing and being added to.

The Spelling section is split into two parts. First, to help you to spell correctly, there are some spelling rules and strategies. The second part is an alphabetical word list, with the word class and word forms in full so that you can look up words and check all their spellings easily. There are also tips to help you to avoid making common spelling errors.

Vowels and consonants

The letters **a**, **e**, **i**, **o** and **u** are called **vowels**. Nearly all words contain at least one vowel. They can make a short vowel sound or a long vowel sound. All other letters are called **consonants**.

How to spell the long vowel sounds

There are different ways of writing sounds. They are usually shown between two forward slashes, e.g. /i/. This dictionary uses the International Phonetic Alphabet (IPA).

a   /eɪ/ sounds like 'play'

Different ways of spelling this sound:

ai	wait	rain
ay	day	play
a_e	cake	same
a	acorn	angel
-ey	grey	they
ea	great	break

WATCH OUT
Other letter groups can also make this sound. The **eigh** in **eight**, the **ei** in **vein** and the **ae** in **sundae** all make this sound.

VOWEL SOUNDS

e /iː/ sounds like 'tree'

Different ways of spelling this sound:

ee	sweet	peel	see
e_e	compete	theme	
ey	monkey	keys	
ie	thief	field	
ei	ceiling	receive	
ea	meat	deal	sea
i_e	sardine		

Words that are exceptions!
were   here   there
where   friend   eye

⚠ WATCH OUT

This sound can be made by both ie and ei. The general rule for this is 'i before e, except after c'.
believe   **receive**

Words that are exceptions!   protein   caffeine   seize

A very similar sound is also made by the letter **y** at the end of a word.
baby   happy   completely   secondary   candy

---

i /aɪ/ sounds like 'high'

Different ways of spelling this sound:

igh	light	bright	fright
ie	cried	pie	tie
i_e	five	despite	alike
i	behind	mind	idle
ui	guide	disguise	

⚠ WATCH OUT

This sound can also be made by the letter **y**.
my   by   fly   reply   deny   bypass
In **height**, **ei** makes this sound.

o /əʊ/ sounds like 'road'

Different ways of spelling this sound:

oa	boat	toast
o	so	go
o_e	broke	hole
oe	woe	toe
ow	tow	own
eau	plateau	gateau
ough	although	dough

Words that are exceptions!
love   come   some
one   once

WATCH OUT
Lots of words are spelt with the letters **-ough** and they can make different sounds. See page 135 for more information.

u /u:/ sounds like 'moon'

Different ways of spelling this sound:

oo	zoo	spoon
ue	clue	true
u_e	flute	rude
ew	crew	flew
o	to	who
ou	you	soup
ough	through	
ui	bruise	fruit
u	super	truth

WATCH OUT
If a word ends in this sound, it is more likely to end in either **ue** or **ew** than **oo**.

u — **/juː/ sounds like 'tube'**

Different ways of spelling this sound:

ue	argue
ew	knew
u_e	cube
eu	feud
you	youth
u	university tuna

More vowel sounds

sound	examples					
/ʊ/	book	could	push			
/aː/	car	father	palm			
/ɔː/	fork	saw	your	saucer	oar	floor
	more	war	reward	towards	naughty	brought
	warm	quarter	water	walk		
/ɜː/	turn	her	bird	early	word	
	heard	learn	search	rehearse	yearn	
/aʊ/	clown	found	plough			
/ɔɪ/	coin	toy				
/ɪə/	hear	ear	sphere	pier	deer	
/eə/	chair	care	bear	there	pear	swear
/jʊə/	cure					
/ɪ/	biscuit	circuit	guilty	gym	mystery	
	cymbal	typical				
/jɔː/	your	yourself				

Making nouns plural

Words like **girl**, **book**, **school** and **year** are all nouns. One of their main jobs is to identify a person, place or thing. If you are talking about just one item, this is **singular**. More than one item is **plural**.

To make most nouns plural, add **-s**.

apple + **s** = apple**s**   dog + **s** = dog**s**   computer + **s** = computer**s**

girl + **s** = girl**s**   book + **s** = book**s**   school + **s** = school**s**

year + **s** = year**s**

If the noun ends in **-s**, **-ss**, **-x**, **-sh** or **-ch**, add **-es**.

bus + **es** = bus**es**   glass + **es** = glass**es**   fox + **es** = fox**es**

brush + **es** = brush**es**   watch + **es** = watch**es**

If the noun ends in a consonant + **-y**, change the **-y** to **ie** then add **-s**.

baby + **ie** + s = bab**ies**   body + **ie** + s = bod**ies**

family + **ie** + s = famil**ies**   strawberry + **ie** + s = strawberr**ies**

PLURALS

If the noun ends in a single **-f** or **-fe**, change the **-f** or **-fe** to **-ves**.

half + **ves** = hal**ves**   life + **ves** = li**ves**   knife + **ves** = kni**ves**
self + **ves** = sel**ves**   scarf + **ves** = scar**ves**   wife + **ves** = wi**ves**

If the noun ends in **-o**, add **-es**.

hero + **es** = hero**es**   tomato + **es** = tomato**es**   potato + **es** = potato**es**

> **!** **WATCH OUT**
> Some nouns ending in **-f** and **-o** only need an **-s** to make the plural.
>
> roof + **s** = roof**s**   piano + **s** = piano**s**   radio + **s** = radio**s**
>
> Some words ending in **-f** and **-o** can have their plurals in two different ways.
>
> hoof + **s** = hoof**s**   or   hoof + **ves** = hoo**ves**
> halo + **s** = halo**s**   or   halo + **-es** = halo**es**
> cargo + **s** = cargo**s**   or   cargo + **-es** = cargo**es**

More plurals

The plurals of some words are formed in different ways; this is often because these words originally came from languages such as Latin and French where plurals are formed in a different way.

singular	plural	singular	plural
antenna	**antennae**	deer	**deer**
fungus	**fungi**	person	**people**
crisis	**crises**	man	**men**
emphasis	**emphases**	woman	**women**
sheep	**sheep**	child	**children**
penny	**pence** or **pennies**	mouse	**mice**

Adding -ing to verbs

Words like **run**, **jump**, **fly**, and **love** are verbs. Some of them identify an action. Some of them identify a mental process, for example **think**, **feel** and **wonder**. Verbs can also be used to talk about how something appears, for example **seem**, **sound** and **smell**.

When a verb has the ending **-ing**, it tells you that it is in the present tense. This means it is happening at this precise moment, or happening now and continuing to happen.

For most regular verbs, add **-ing** to the infinitive form of the verb.

play + **ing** = play**ing**   wait + **ing** = wait**ing**
listen + **ing** = listen**ing**   work + **ing** = work**ing**

As a general rule, if the infinitive ends in a single vowel + a single consonant, you double the consonant before adding **-ing**.

chop + **p** + **ing** = cho**pp**ing   run + **n** + **ing** = ru**nn**ing

   If the infinitive form has more than one syllable, then the doubling rule generally only applies if the stress is on the last syllable.

forget = forge**tt**ing   develop = developing

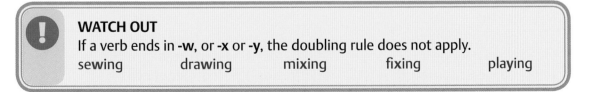

WATCH OUT
The verbs **focus** and **benefit** can either double the final consonant, or just keep the single consonant.

Year 9 students are focu**ss**ing / focusing on their Shakespeare assignments.
We are all benefi**tt**ing / benefiting from the extra funding.

WATCH OUT
If a verb ends in **-w**, or **-x** or **-y**, the doubling rule does not apply.
sewing   drawing   mixing   fixing   playing

! The vowels are a, e, i, o and u; all the other letters are consonants.

> ! If the infinitive ends in a vowel + consonant(s) + **e**, you remove the final **e** and then add **–ing**.
>
> decide + **ing** = deci**ding**   juggle + **ing** = jugg**ling**   tickle + **ing** = tick**ling**
> clothe + **ing** = clo**thing**   smile + **ing** = smi**ling**   race + **ing** = ra**cing**

> If a verb ends in **-ie**, change the **-ie** to **-y** before adding **-ing**.
>
> tie + **y** + **ing** = t**ying**   lie + **y** + **ing** = l**ying**   die + **y** + **ing** = d**ying**

> If a verb ends in **-y**, just add **-ing**.
>
> cry + **ing** = cr**ying**   fly + **ing** = fl**ying**   reply + **ing** = repl**ying**
> copy + **ing** = copy**ing**   carry + **ing** = carry**ing**   stay + **ing** = stay**ing**

Adding -ed to verbs

When a verb has the ending **-ed**, it tells you that it is in the past tense and that the action happened in the past.

> For regular verbs, add **-ed** to make a past tense.
>
> pick + **ed** = pick**ed**   weigh + **ed** = weigh**ed**
> laugh + **ed** = laugh**ed**   whisper + **ed** = whisper**ed**
> happen + **ed** = happen**ed**   stoop + **ed** = stoop**ed**

> As a general rule, if the infinitive ends in a single vowel + a single consonant, you double the consonant and then add **-ed**.
>
> clap + **p** + **ed** = clap**ped**   regret + **t** + **ed** = regret**ted**
> thin + **n** + **ed** = thin**ned**   dip + **p** + **ed** = dip**ped**
> log + **g** + **ed** = log**ged**   rot + **t** + **ed** = rot**ted**
> scrub + **b** + **ed** = scrub**bed**   stop + **p** + **ed** = stop**ped**

SPELLING

If the verb ends in a vowel + consonant(s) + **e**, just add **d**.

smile + **d** = smil**ed**   hike + **d** = hik**ed**
poke + **d** = pok**ed**   tickle + **d** = tickl**ed**

If the verb ends in a consonant + **-y**, change the **-y** to **-i** and add **-ed**.

cr~~y~~ + **i** + **ed** = cr**ied**   cop~~y~~ + **i** + **ed** = cop**ied**   carr~~y~~ + **i** + **ed** = carr**ied**

If the verb ends in a vowel + **-y**, just add **-ed**.

play + **ed** = play**ed**   stay + **ed** = stay**ed**   obey + **ed** = obey**ed**

If the verb ends in **-ie**, just add **-d**.

tie + **d** = tie**d**   lie + **d** = lie**d**

!

WATCH OUT
Some irregular verbs do not add **-ed** to form the past tense.
See page 20 for a list of irregular verbs and their past tenses.

lay → **laid**   pay → **paid**   say → **said**

fly → **flew**   feed → **fed**   take → **took**

! The vowels are a, e, i, o and u; all the other letters are consonants.

Adding -er and -est to adjectives

Adjectives are words like **big**, **excited**, **blue** and **surprised**. They describe things that are named by nouns. Adjectives can compare and contrast things. For most adjectives, if you are comparing two things, add **-er** to the adjective. This is called the **comparative**. For most adjectives, if you are comparing more than two things, add **-est**. This is called the **superlative**.

adjective	comparative form	superlative form
long	longer	longest
fast	faster	fastest
slow	slower	slowest
small	smaller	smallest
quick	quicker	quickest
short	shorter	shortest

However, if the adjective ends in **-e**, just add **-r** or **-st**.

adjective	comparative form	superlative form
rude	ruder	rudest
huge	huger	hugest
nice	nicer	nicest

If the adjective has a short vowel sound and ends in a consonant, double the consonant before adding **-er** or **-est**.

adjective	comparative form	superlative form
hot	hotter	hottest
fit	fitter	fittest
big	bigger	biggest

SPELLING

If the adjective ends in a consonant + **-y**, change the **-y** to **-i** before adding **-er** or **-est**.

adjective	comparative form	superlative form
funny	funn**ier**	funn**iest**
shiny	shin**ier**	shin**iest**
wobbly	wobbl**ier**	wobbl**iest**
tidy	tid**ier**	tid**iest**

For some adjectives with two syllables, you can use either **more** or **most** before the adjective, or add **-er** or **–est** to make the comparative or superlative forms.

✔ Ismail is much **more clever** than I am.

✔ Ismail is much **cleverer** than me.

✔ Anna is the **most clever** girl in our year.

✔ Anna is the **cleverest** girl in our year.

For adjectives with three or more syllables and adjectives ending in **-ful**, **-less**, **-ing**, **-ed** or **-ous**, do not add **-er** or **-est**.

For these adjectives, always use **more** or **most** in front of them.

✔ Going skiing was one of the **most incredible** experiences of my life.

✘ Going skiing was one of the **incrediblest** experiences of my life.

✔ That was the **most frightening** film I have ever seen!

✘ That was the **frighteningest** film I have ever seen!

! The vowels are a, e, i, o and u; all the other letters are consonants.

More adjectives which take **more** or **most**:

adjective	comparative form	superlative form
alive	**more** alive	**most** alive
awful	**more** awful	**most** awful
certain	**more** certain	**most** certain
correct	**more** correct	**most** correct
enormous	**more** enormous	**most** enormous
excellent	**more** excellent	**most** excellent
freezing	**more** freezing	**most** freezing
furious	**more** furious	**most** furious
gigantic	**more** gigantic	**most** gigantic
immediate	**more** immediate	**most** immediate
important	**more** important	**most** important
minuscule	**more** minuscule	**most** minuscule
overjoyed	**more** overjoyed	**most** overjoyed
perfect	**more** perfect	**most** perfect
ridiculous	**more** ridiculous	**most** ridiculous
special	**more** special	**most** special
superb	**more** superb	**most** superb
terrible	**more** terrible	**most** terrible
unknown	**more** unknown	**most** unknown

Adding -ly to adjectives

Add **-ly** to an adjective to make it into an adverb. Adverbs modify verbs, adjectives, other adverbs or whole sentences.

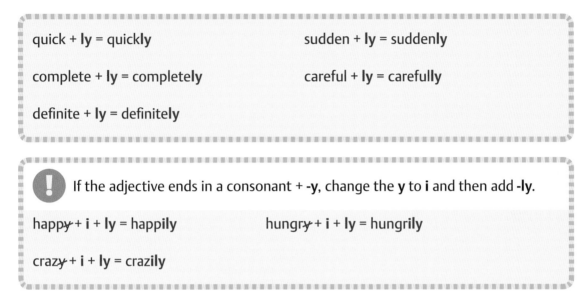

quick + **ly** = quick**ly**

complete + **ly** = complete**ly**

definite + **ly** = definite**ly**

sudden + **ly** = sudden**ly**

careful + **ly** = careful**ly**

! If the adjective ends in a consonant + **-y**, change the **y** to **i** and then add **-ly**.

happ~~y~~ + **i** + **ly** = happ**ily**

craz~~y~~ + **i** + **ly** = craz**ily**

hungr~~y~~ + **i** + **ly** = hungr**ily**

Prefixes

A **prefix** is a group of letters that can be added to the beginning of the base or root form of a word. Prefixes are useful because you can use them to vary your vocabulary and to create new words.

Different prefixes have different meanings so, when you add a prefix to a word, you change its meaning and make a new word.

dis + appear = **dis**appear   **im** + possible = **im**possible

un + well = **un**well   **sub** + marine = **sub**marine

prefix	meaning	examples	
re-	again	recycle	reuse
pre-	before	prehistoric	premeditated
ex-	out, outside of	export	exit
co-	together	cooperate	coordinate
anti-	against	antiseptic	anti-hero
auto-	self	automatic	autobiography
circum-	round, about	circumference	circumnavigate
bi-	two, twice	bicycle	bicentenary
tele-	at a distance	telephone	telepathy
trans-	across	transport	transatlantic
pro-	supporting	pro-hunting	pro-government
sub-	below	submarine	substandard
inter-	between, among	international	intersperse
super-	above, over, beyond	superman	supersize
over-	excessively	overused	overexcited

Some prefixes make the opposite of the root word.

prefix	meaning	examples
un-	not or the opposite of	unwell
de-	undoing or taking away	de-stress
dis-	not	dishonest
dis-	opposite of	disappear
mis-	wrong	misbehave
non-	not	non-stop
im- / ir- / il-	not	impossible irregular illegal

WATCH OUT
The prefix **in-** can mean both **not** and **in** or **into**.

inedible = not edible   **in**doors = inside (your house)

Some words just begin with the same letters of a prefix. You can spot these words easily by taking away the prefix and seeing whether you are left with a base form or root word.

reply   innocent   reach   receive   discuss

Hyphens can be used to join a prefix to a root word.

co-own   re-enter   de-stress   non-stop

Suffixes

A **suffix** is a group of letters that can be added to the end of the base or root form of a word.

Different suffixes have different meanings so, when you add a suffix to a word, you change its meaning and make a new word.

speak + **er** = speak**er**

sad + **ness** = sad**ness**

joy + **ful** = joy**ful**

hope + **less** = hope**less**

---

suffix	meaning	examples	
-er	a person or thing that does something	runner	entertainer
-less	not having	wireless	hopeless
-able	able to be done	likeable	doable
-hood	a particular state or condition	childhood	
-ness	a particular state or condition	kindness	

If you are adding **-er** to a word which ends in a single vowel and single consonant, double the consonant and then add the suffix.

run + **n** + **er** = run**n**er

cut + **t** + **er** = cut**t**er

! **–er** and **–est** are added to some adjectives to make the comparative and superlative forms. For more about this, see page 118.

More words end in **-able** than **-ible**. A useful way to check your spelling is to see if you have a root word (a word that makes sense on its own) left after taking off the **-able**. If not, then the ending is **-ible**.

✔ eat~~able~~ = eat

✘ poss~~ible~~ = poss

> For some words that end in **-y**, take the **-y** away before adding **-able**.
>
> miser~~y~~+ **able** = miser**able**
>
> For other words that end in **-y**, change the **-y** to **-i** before adding **-able**.
>
> env~~y~~+ **i** + **able** = env**iable**

Some suffixes can change a word into a different **word class**.

teach (verb)	+ **er**	= teach**er** (noun)
apolog~~y~~ (noun)	+ **ize**	= apolog**ize** (verb)
quick (adjective)	+ **ly**	= quick**ly** (adverb)

These suffixes change **verbs** into **nouns**.

suffix	meaning	verb	noun
-er	a person or thing that does something	teach	teach**er**
-or	a person or thing that does something	act	act**or**
-ment	nouns of action or purpose	enjoy	enjoy**ment**
-ant / -ent	someone who does something	attend	attend**ant**
-tion / -ation	nouns of action or condition	direct inform	direc**tion** inform**ation**

These suffixes can be combined with **nouns** to make **adjectives**.

suffix	meaning	noun	adjective
-ous	characterized by	danger	danger**ous**
-ful	full of	play	play**ful**
-less	not having / without	fear	fear**less**

Spelling different word endings

-ion or -ian?

For root words ending in **-t** or **-te**, use **-tion**.

collect + **tion** = collec**tion**   loca~~te~~ + **tion** = loca**tion**

For root words ending in **-ss** or **-mit**, use **-ssion**.

posse~~ss~~ + **ssion** = posse**ssion**   permi~~t~~ + **ssion** = permi**ssion**

For root words ending in **-d**, **-de** or **-se**, use **-sion**.

expan~~d~~ + **sion** = expan**sion**   deci~~de~~ + **sion** = deci**sion**
preci~~se~~ + **sion** = preci**sion**   revi~~se~~ + **sion** = revi**sion**

WATCH OUT
Words that are exceptions!
intend → intention   attend → attention

For root words ending in **-c** or **-cs**, use **-cian**.

magi~~c~~ + **cian** = magi**cian**   politi~~cs~~ + **cian** = politi**cian**

-ent or -ant?

-ent, **-ence** or **-ency** often follow a **soft c**, **soft g** or **qu**

innoc**ent** → innoc**ence**   intellig**ent** → intellig**ence**

Use **-ant**, **-ance** or **-ancy** if you know there is a related word that ends in **-ation**.

hesit**ation**   →   hesit**ant**   →   hesit**ancy**
toler**ation**   →   toler**ant**   →   toler**ance**
observ**ation** →   observ**ant** →   observ**ance**

> Words that are exceptions!
> assist**ant** → assist**ance**   obedi**ent** → obedi**ence**   independ**ent** → independ**ence**

-cial or -tial?

You often use **-cial** after a vowel.

spe**cial**   so**cial**   offi**cial**

You often use **-tial** after a consonant.

essen**tial**   par**tial**   presiden**tial**

> **! WATCH OUT**
> There are lots of exceptions.
> commer**cial**   finan**cial**   ini**tial**   pala**tial**   spa**tial**

-cious or -tious?

You usually use **-cious** if the root word ends in **-ce**. For other words, use **–tious**.

spa**ce** → spa**cious**   cau**tion** → cau**tious**
gra**ce** → gra**cious**   infect   → infec**tious**

-sure, -ture or -cher?

Say the word carefully, thinking about the sound the ending makes. The sound at the end of these words is spelt **-sure**.

trea**sure**	plea**sure**	mea**sure**	lei**sure**

The sound at the end of these words is spelt **-ture**.

pic**ture**	adven**ture**	mix**ture**	tempera**ture**
fu**ture**	struc**ture**	fix**ture**	crea**ture**

This sound can also be spelt **-cher**.

ar**cher**	but**cher**	sear**cher**	stret**cher**
tea**cher**	ri**cher**	cat**cher**	vou**cher**

Using apostrophes

Apostrophes can show when a word has been made shorter by dropping one or more letters. This is called a **contraction**.

I **am** = I'm   did **not** = didn't   could **not** = couldn't   we **are** = we're

---

! WATCH OUT
Be careful not to confuse:

we're and were

We're all really fed up with this.	The word **we're** is a contraction of **we are**.
What **were** you doing in the park?	The word **were** is a past tense form of the verb **to be**.

they're, their and there

They're going to the house.	The word **they're** is a contraction of **they are**.
It is **their** house.	The word **their** means **belonging to them**.
There is the house.	The word **there** shows **place** or **position**.

SPELLING

! **WATCH OUT**

it's and its

It's really busy in town.

It's been raining all morning.

The peregrine had two eggs in **its** nest.

The word **it's** is a contraction of **it is**.

The word **it's** is a contraction of **it has**.

The word **its** is a determiner meaning **belonging to it**.

who's and whose

Who's going to the party on Saturday?

Who's finished their work?

I went to meet Simon Jones, **whose** father owns the factory.

The word **who's** is a contraction of **who is**.

The word **who's** is a contraction of **who has**.

The word **whose** is a relative pronoun meaning **belonging to the person or thing just mentioned**.

you're and your

You're the only person I can trust.

Don't forget **your** bus pass!

The word **you're** is a contraction of **you are**.

Your is a determiner meaning **belonging to you**.

Apostrophes are also used to show when someone or something owns something. For most of these nouns you add an **apostrophe** followed by an **-s**.

Tom**'s** trains   The trains belong to Tom.

The dog**'s** bowl   The bowl belongs to the dog.

When the noun already ends in **-s**, just add an apostrophe. For more, see page 105.

The birds' wings   The wings belong to more than one bird.

! **WATCH OUT**

If you are using a noun which is plural remember that some plurals are irregular and don't end in **-s**. For some of these, add an **apostrophe** + **-s**.

children's playground   women's coats

Homophones

Homophones are words that have the same pronunciation but different meanings, origins and spelling.

Because homophones sound exactly the same, it is easy to get them confused.

new	knew	no	know
right	write	through	threw
hole	whole	great	grate
for	four, fore	heard	herd
see	sea	be	bee
blue	blew	bare	bear
one	won	cheap	cheep
night	knight	hear	here
vain	vein, vane	currant	current
dessert	desert	yolk	yoke

! If you are not sure which homophone to use in a particular sentence, check both spellings in a dictionary.

Homographs

Homographs are words that are spelt the same way but not necessarily pronounced the same way and have different meanings and origins.

These examples show homographs that are spelt the same way but are pronounced differently:

Samira was captain of the school **rowing** team.
Mum said she was sick of us **rowing** about the laptop.

Jesse tied a **bow** round the bottom of the tree.
The audience cheered as the dancers took a **bow**.

She watched in horror as a **tear** rolled down Sasha's cheek.
Tear the form off and send it to the address below.

Make sure you **wind** the flex up neatly.
The leaves fluttered in the **wind**.

These homographs are spelt and pronounced the same:

The price of school dinners **rose** five per cent on average last year.
The ball went over the fence and landed in the **rose** bushes.

We could hear the **crickets** from our room.
The boys play **cricket** in the summer.

Swallows migrate south in summer.
I drank my water in five big **swallows**.

I can see **mould** on that apple.
Pour the jelly into the **mould** and refrigerate for an hour.

Silent letters

Some words have silent letters in them which make them tricky to spell.
Try to learn these spellings.

In the following words:

silent **l** follows vowels **a, o** and **ou**	ta**l**k	cha**l**k	ca**l**m	ha**l**f	ca**l**f	sa**l**mon
	yo**l**k	fo**l**k	shou**l**d	wou**l**d	cou**l**d	
silent **b** follows **m**	plum**b**	dum**b**	num**b**	bom**b**	tom**b**	lam**b**
	thum**b**	crum**b**	wom**b**			
silent **b** comes before **t**	de**b**t	dou**b**t				
silent **k** comes before **n**	**k**now	**k**neel	**k**not	**k**nock	**k**night	**k**nife
	knickers	**k**nit	**k**nee	**k**nuckle		
silent **g** comes before **n**	**g**nome	**g**nat	**g**naw	**g**narled		
silent **n** follows **m**	solem**n**	colum**n**				
silent **w** comes before **r**	**w**rite	**w**rong	**w**rist	**w**reck	**w**retch	**w**rench
	wrestle	**w**rapper				
silent **p** comes before **s** or **n**	**p**salm	**p**neumatic	**p**sychology		**p**sychiatrist	
	pneumonia					
silent **h** follows **w**, **c** or **r**	w**h**eat	w**h**ale	w**h**ine	w**h**irl	w**h**en	w**h**y
	w**h**ere	w**h**at	c**h**emist	c**h**ord	r**h**ino	r**h**ubarb

> **!** **WATCH OUT**
> The words s**w**ord and ans**w**er also have a silent **w**.
>
> Some words start with a silent **h**.
> **h**onest   **h**our   **h**eir   **h**onour

SPELLING

More spelling rules

soft g and soft c

When a **g** or a **c** is followed by **i**, **e** or **y**:

- the **g** usually sounds like the letter **j**   **gi**raffe   **ge**rm   **gy**m
- the **c** becomes a **/s/** sound   **ci**rcus   **ce**ntre   **cy**cle

how to spell /dʒ/, sounds like 'jump'

This sound can be spelt using the letter **j**   **j**og   **j**ar   ad**j**ust

This sound can also be spelt using:

- the letter group **ge**   a**ge**   hu**ge**   chan**ge**
- after a short vowel sound, the letter group **dge**

  ba**dge**   do**dge**   e**dge**
- A **y** can make the letter **g** sound like a **j**:   **g**ym   biolo**gy**   apolo**gy**

y can make the /ɪ/ sound, as in 'myth'

Sometimes the letter **y** sounds like the short /ɪ/ sound.

gym   mystery   cymbal   system   syllable   typical   rhythm

133

a can make the /ɒ/ sound, sounds like 'watch'

Usually the letter **a** can sound like the short o vowel when it has a **w** in front of it.

was	s**wa**mp	**wa**sp	s**wa**llow	**wa**nder	s**wa**t	**wa**nt
s**wa**n	**wa**sh	**wa**tch	**wa**llet			

ar can make the /ɔ:(r)/ sound

Usually the letter group **ar** can sound like **or** when it has a **w** in front of it.

war	s**wa**rm	**wa**rn	re**wa**rd	to**wa**rds

que can sound like /k/

-que is pronounced /k/ when it occurs at the end of a word.

anti**que**   uni**que**

gue can sound like /g/

-gue is pronounced /g/ when it occurs at the end of a word.

dialo**gue**   lea**gue**

More tricky letters

- The letter group **ch** sometimes makes a /k/ sound.

  s**ch**ool   **ch**orus   **ch**emist

- The letter group **ch** sometimes sound like the letter group **sh**.

  chateau   **ch**ef   bro**ch**ure

- The letter group **ph** usually sounds like the letter **f**.

  phrase   **ph**otogra**ph**

- The letter group **sc** sometimes sounds like the letter **s**.

  science   **sc**ene   fa**sc**inate

the sounds made by the letter group **ough**

Lots of words are spelt with the letter group **ough**, but they can sound very different from each other. Many of these words are frequently used, so it is important to learn the correct spellings.

/ɔː/ sound	/əʊ/ sound	/uː/ sound	/ə/ sound	/aʊ/ sound	/ɒf/ sound
ought	th**ough**	thr**ough**	thor**ough**	pl**ough**	c**ough**
f**ough**t	alth**ough**		bor**ough**	b**ough**	tr**ough**
b**ough**t	d**ough**				
th**ough**t					
n**ough**t					

WATCH OUT
The letter group **ough** can make the /ʌf/ sound.
r**ough**   t**ough**   en**ough**

the sounds made by the letter group ou

Lots of words are spelt with the letter group **ou**, but they can sound very different from each other. Many of these words are frequently used, so it is important to learn the correct spellings.

/aʊ/ sound	/uː/ sound	/ɔː(r)/ sound	/ʌ/ sound
out	you	four	young
house	group	pour	double
mouse		your	trouble
about			

the endings el, le or al

-le is a more common ending than **-el** and **-al**, especially in two-syllable words.

The ending **-le** often comes after a letter with an ascender (**b, d, k**).
able   middle   candle   chuckle

The ending **-le** is also often preceded by letters with a descender (**y, g**).
giggle   angle   style

The ending **-le** comes after a hard **c** or hard **g** sound:
uncle   giggle   angle

The ending **-el** often comes after **m, n, r, s, v, w** or after a soft **c** or soft **g** sound.
camel   tunnel   squirrel   tinsel   travel   towel
parcel   angel

The ending **-al** often comes after **d, b, d** or **t**.
pedal   cannibal   medal   metal   petal

Become a better speller!

Some of the most frequently used words in the English language, such as **does**, **accidentally**, **different**, **definitely** and **usually**, are hard to spell because they are not written the way they sound or do not fit in with regular spelling rules.

Here are some tips to help you improve your spelling.

- Set yourself targets. Choose one or two words to focus on and use one of the strategies below to help you remember how to get them right next time.

- Some words can be hard to spell because they have 'hidden' syllables. For example, we don't usually pronounce the **e** in the middle of **different** or the **a** in the middle of **actually**. Try to find words in the same family that reveal missing vowels.

Some frequently used words with hidden syllables:

different	actually	chocolate	realize	probably
favourite	every	accidentally	medicine	

- Words like **because** and **does** are hard to spell because it is impossible to guess how to spell the vowel sound in them. For words like these, it can be useful to learn a mnemonic or rhyme. The sillier they are, the easier they are to remember.

because	Big elephants can always understand small elephants.
does	Ducks often eat snails.
rhythm	Rhythm helps your two hips move.
separate	There's a rat in separate.
quiet	Please keep quiet about my diet.

- Try learning words in families. Word families are related to each other by spelling, grammar and meaning. When you know how to spell one member of the family, you can use it to help spell other words.

write	→	writer	→	writing	→	rewrite
noise	→	noisy	→	noiseless		
photograph	→	photographer	→	photographic		
danger	→	dangerous	→	dangerously		

Dictionary — How to use this dictionary

alphabet
The alphabet is on every page with the letter you are in highlighted, so you can find your way around the dictionary quickly and easily.

catch words
These are the first and last words on the page; they will guide you to the correct place to find the words you need.

headword
in alphabetical order, it shows you how to spell the word

Try also
This note helps you to check in other parts of the dictionary to find your word.

word class
what type of word the headword is, for example, noun, verb, adjective or adverb

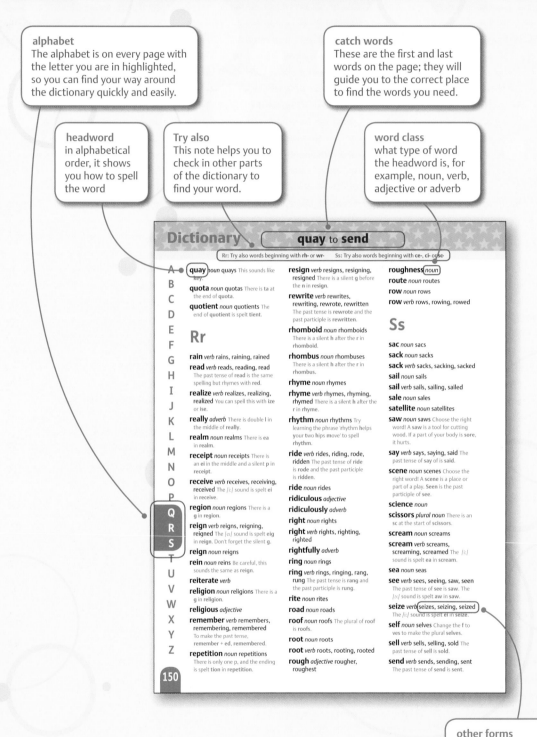

Dictionary   quay to send

Rr: Try also words beginning with **rh-** or **wr-**   Ss: Try also words beginning with **ce-**, **ci-** or **sc-**

A B C D E F G H I J K L M N O P Q R S T U V W X Y Z

150

quay *noun* quays This sounds like key.

quota *noun* quotas There is **ta** at the end of **quota**.

quotient *noun* quotients The end of **quotient** is spelt **tient**.

Rr

rain *verb* rains, raining, rained

read *verb* reads, reading, read The past tense of **read** is the same spelling but rhymes with red.

realize *verb* realizes, realizing, realized You can spell this with **ize** or **ise**.

really *adverb* There is double **l** in the middle of **really**.

realm *noun* realms There is **ea** in **realm**.

receipt *noun* receipts There is an **ei** in the middle and a silent **p** in **receipt**.

receive *verb* receives, receiving, received The /iː/ sound is spelt **ei** in **receive**.

region *noun* regions There is a **g** in **region**.

reign *verb* reigns, reigning, reigned The /eɪ/ sound is spelt **eig** in **reign**. Don't forget the silent **g**.

reign *noun* reigns

rein *noun* reins Be careful, this sounds the same as **reign**.

reiterate *verb*

religion *noun* religions There is a **g** in **religion**.

religious *adjective*

remember *verb* remembers, remembering, remembered To make the past tense, remember + ed, remembered.

repetition *noun* repetitions There is only one **p**, and the ending is spelt **tion** in **repetition**.

resign *verb* resigns, resigning, resigned There is a silent **g** before the **n** in **resign**.

rewrite *verb* rewrites, rewriting, rewrote, rewritten The past tense is **rewrote** and the past participle is **rewritten**.

rhomboid *noun* rhomboids There is a silent **h** after the **r** in **rhomboid**.

rhombus *noun* rhombuses There is a silent **h** after the **r** in **rhombus**.

rhyme *noun* rhymes

rhyme *verb* rhymes, rhyming, rhymed There is a silent **h** after the **r** in **rhyme**.

rhythm *noun* rhythms Try learning the phrase 'rhythm helps your two hips move' to spell **rhythm**.

ride *verb* rides, riding, rode, ridden The past tense of **ride** is **rode** and the past participle is **ridden**.

ride *noun* rides

ridiculous *adjective*

ridiculously *adverb*

right *noun* rights

right *verb* rights, righting, righted

rightfully *adverb*

ring *noun* rings

ring *verb* rings, ringing, rang, rung The past tense is **rang** and the past participle is **rung**.

rite *noun* rites

road *noun* roads

roof *noun* roofs The plural of **roof** is **roofs**.

root *noun* roots

root *verb* roots, rooting, rooted

rough *adjective* rougher, roughest

roughness *noun*

route *noun* routes

row *noun* rows

row *verb* rows, rowing, rowed

Ss

sac *noun* sacs

sack *noun* sacks

sack *verb* sacks, sacking, sacked

sail *noun* sails

sail *verb* sails, sailing, sailed

sale *noun* sales

satellite *noun* satellites

saw *noun* saws Choose the right word! A **saw** is a tool for cutting wood. If a part of your body is **sore**, it hurts.

say *verb* says, saying, said The past tense of **say** is **said**.

scene *noun* scenes Choose the right word! A **scene** is a place or part of a play. **Seen** is the past participle of **see**.

science *noun*

scissors *plural noun* There is an **sc** at the start of **scissors**.

scream *noun* screams

scream *verb* screams, screaming, screamed The /iː/ sound is spelt **ea** in **scream**.

sea *noun* seas

see *verb* sees, seeing, saw, seen The past tense of **see** is **saw**. The /ɔː/ sound is spelt **aw** in **saw**.

seize *verb* seizes, seizing, seized The /iː/ sound is spelt **ei** in **seize**.

self *noun* selves Change the **f** to **ves** to make the plural **selves**.

sell *verb* sells, selling, sold The past tense of **sell** is **sold**.

send *verb* sends, sending, sent The past tense of **send** is **sent**.

other forms
The different forms of the word are also given so that you can see how to spell the word with different endings.

Aa

abolition *noun* The end of **abolition** is spelt **tion**.

absolute *adjective*

absolutely *adverb* Absolutely = absolute + ly. Don't forget to keep the **e** after the **t**.

acceleration *noun* Remember that the beginning is spelt **acc** and the ending is spelt **tion**. Do not forget that there is only one **l**.

accept *verb* accepts, accepting, accepted

accident *noun* accidents

accidentally *adverb* Accidentally = accident + ally. Don't forget the **a** and the double **l** before the **y**.

accommodation *noun* There is a double **c** and a double **m** in **accommodation**.

accompany *verb* accompanies, accompanying, accompanied

account *noun* accounts There is a double **c** in **account**.

accumulation *noun* accumulations Remember that there is a double **c**, and the ending is spelt **tion**.

ache *noun* aches

ache *verb* aches, aching, ached

achievement *noun* achievements There is an **ie** in **achievement**.

actually *adverb*

address *noun* addresses There is a double **d** and a double **s** in **address**.

address *verb* addresses, addressing, addressed

adjacent *adjective* There is a **d** before the **j**, and the /s/ sound is spelt with a **c** in **adjacent**.

advice *noun*

advise *verb* advises, advising, advised Choose the right word! **Advice** is a noun and **advise** is a verb, e.g. *She gave me some good advice* and *I advise you to forget the whole thing.*

affect *verb* affects, affecting, affected Be careful, **affect** and **effect** are easy to confuse.

affection *noun* affections

again *adverb* The end of **again** is spelt **ain**.

aging *adjective*

air *noun* airs

air *verb* airs, airing, aired

aisle *noun* aisles

algebra *noun* There is a **g** in **algebra**.

algorithm *noun* algorithms There is an **i** after the **r**, and no vowel between the **h** and the **m**.

alliteration *noun* There is a double **l** in **alliteration**, and only one **t** before the **er**.

allow *verb* allows, allowing, allowed Choose the right word! **Allowed** means to be permitted to do something, e.g. *Running in the corridors is not allowed.* **Aloud** means in a voice that can be heard, e.g. *He read the letter aloud.*

all right *adjective, interjection* Although **all right** can be spelt **alright**, you should use **all right** in formal writing.

aloud *adverb*

altar *noun* altars

alter *verb* alters, altering, altered

although *conjunction* There is only one **l** in **although**.

altogether *adverb* There is only one **l** in **altogether**.

ambiguous *adjective* Do not forget the **u** before the **ous** in **ambiguous**.

ambitious *adjective*

analyse *verb* analyses, analysing, analysed

ancestor *noun* ancestors

ancient *adjective*

animation *noun* animations The ending of **animation** is spelt **tion**.

answer *noun* answers

answer *verb* answers, answering, answered There is a silent **w** in **answer**.

antenna *noun* The plural of **antenna** is **antennae**.

antique *noun* antiques

anxious *adjective*

appear *verb* appears, appearing, appeared There is a double **p** in **appear**.

appearance *noun* appearances

application *noun* applications The ending of **application** is spelt **tion**. Do not forget the double **p**.

appreciate *verb* appreciates, appreciating, appreciated

approach *verb* approaches, approaching, approached There is a double **p** in **approach**.

approach *noun* approaches

archive *noun* archives The /k/ sound is spelt **ch** in **archive**.

are *verb*

area *noun* areas

aren't Aren't = are + not. Add an **apostrophe** between the **n** and the **t**.

argue *verb* argues, arguing, argued There is no **e** in **arguing**.

argument *noun* arguments There is no **e** after the **u** in **argument**.

A B C D E F G H I J K L M N O P Q R S T U V W X Y Z

A

arrive *verb* arrives, arriving, arrived There is a double **r** in **arrive**.

artificial *adjective*

ascent *noun* ascents

assent *noun* assents

assent *verb* assents, assenting, assented Do not forget the double **s** in **assent**.

assistant *noun* assistants

assume *verb* assumes, assuming, assumed

astronaut *noun* astronauts

asymmetric *adjective* There is a **y** before the double **m** in **asymmetric**.

atmosphere *noun* atmospheres

attach *verb* attaches, attaching, attached There is no **t** before the **ch** in **attach**. Do not forget the double **t** at the beginning.

attachment *noun* attachments

attention *noun*

attitude *noun* attitudes There is **tu** in **attitude**. Do not forget the double **t** at the beginning.

audience *noun* audiences

author *noun* authors

authority *noun* authorities

available *adjective*

average *noun* averages

awhile *adverb*

awkward *adjective*

Bb

bail *noun* bails

bail *verb* bails, bailing, bailed

balance *noun* balances

balance *verb* balances, balancing, balanced

bale *noun* bales

bale *verb* bales, baling, baled

balloon *noun* balloons There is a double **l** and a double **o** in **balloon**.

bare *adjective* barer, barest

base *noun* bases

base *verb* bases, basing, based

bass *noun* basses

bathe *verb* bathes, bathing, bathed Bathe with an **e** sounds like **b-ay-the**.

bathe *noun*

beach *noun* beaches

bear *verb* bears, bearing, bore, born or borne

bear *noun* bears

beautiful *adjective* The /juː/ sound in **beautiful** is spelt eau.

beauty *noun* beauties

because *conjunction* To spell **because** try remembering: **b**ig **e**lephants **c**an **a**lways **u**nderstand **s**mall **e**lephants.

beech *noun* beeches

before *adverb, preposition* Before ends with an **e**.

beginning *noun* beginnings Begin + ning = beginning. Don't forget to double the **n** in the middle.

belief *noun* beliefs The /iː/ sound is spelt **ie** in **belief**.

believe *verb* believes, believing, believed Believe ends with ieve.

bet *noun* bets

bet *verb* bets, betting, bet The past tense of **bet** is **bet**.

beware *verb* Beware has no other forms; it is only ever used as an imperative.

bicycle *noun* bicycles

biscuit *noun* biscuits The /ɪ/ sound is spelt **ui** in **biscuit**.

bite *verb* bites, biting, bit, bitten The past tense of bite is **bit**; do not add **ed**.

bite *noun* bites

blew *verb* Blew is the past tense of **blow**.

blow *noun* blows

blow *verb* blows, blowing, blew

blue *adjective* bluer, bluest Choose the right word! **Blue** is a colour. **Blew** is the past tense of **blow**. *The sky was blue. The wind blew hard.*

blue *noun* blues

board *noun* boards

board *verb* boards, boarding, boarded

bomb *noun* bombs

bomb *verb* bombs, bombing, bombed

bored *adjective*

borough *noun* boroughs

boulder *noun* boulders

boundary *noun* boundaries Do not forget the **ary** at the end of **boundary**.

bow *noun* bows

bow *verb* bows, bowing, bowed

brake *noun* brakes

break *verb* breaks, breaking, broke, broken The past tense of **break** is **broke**, e.g. *I broke it.*

break *noun* breaks

breath *noun* breaths

breathe *verb* breathes, breathing, breathed Breathe with an **e** at the end sounds like **br-ee-the**.

bridal *adjective*

bridge *noun* bridges

bridle *noun* bridles

A B C D E F G H I J K L M N O P Q R S T U V W X Y Z

bright *adjective* brighter, brightest

brochure *noun* brochures

bruise *noun* bruises The /uː/ sound is spelt **ui** in **bruise**.

bruise *verb* bruises, bruising, bruised

build *verb* builds, building, built The /ɪ/ sound is spelt **ui** in **building**.

building *noun* buildings

bulge *noun* bulges

bulge *verb* bulges, bulging, bulged

bully *verb* bullies, bullying, bullied When you add **ing** to **bully** you keep the **y**, **bullying**.

bully *noun* bullies

bureau *noun* bureaux

burst *verb* bursts, bursting, burst The past tense of **burst** is also **burst**; don't add **ed**.

business *noun* businesses Don't forget, the **i** comes after the **s** in the middle of **bus-i-ness**.

by *preposition*, *adverb*

bye *noun* byes

byte *noun* bytes Be careful, this sounds the same as **bite**.

Cc

cactus *noun* cacti The plural of **cactus** is **cacti**.

calendar *noun* calendars **Calendar** has an **e** in the middle and **ar** at the end.

calm *adjective* calmer, calmest There is a silent **l** in **calm**.

canoe *noun* canoes

canoe *verb* canoes, canoeing, canoed

can't **Can't** = **can** + **not**. Add an **apostrophe** between the **n** and the **t**.

captain *noun* captains

careful *adjective*

carefully *adverb* **Careful** + **ly** = **carefully**. Don't forget the double **l**.

carriage *noun* carriages

cast *verb* casts, casting, cast The past tense of **cast** is also **cast**; don't add **ed**.

cast *noun* casts

catch *verb* catches, catching, caught The past tense of catch is **caught**, and the /ɔː/ sound is spelt **augh**.

catch *noun* catches

cautious *adjective*

cautiously *adverb*

ceiling *noun* ceilings The word **ceiling** starts **cei**.

cell *noun* cells

centilitre *noun* centilitres The /s/ sound is spelt with a **c** in **centilitre**. Do not forget the **re** at the end.

centimetre *noun* centimetres The /s/ sound is spelt with a **c** in **centimetre**. Do not forget the **re** at the end.

centre *noun* centres There is an **re** at the end of **centre**.

centre *verb* centres, centring, centred

cereal *noun* cereals

certain *adjective* **Certain** ends in **ain**.

challenge *verb* challenges, challenging, challenged

challenge *noun* challenges

changeable *adjective*

characteristic *noun* characteristics The /k/ sound is spelt **ch** in **characteristic**.

chemical *noun*

chimney *noun* chimneys

chocolate *noun* chocolates There is an **o** in the middle of **chocolate**, and it ends in **late**.

choose *verb* chooses, choosing, chose, chosen The past tense is **chose** and the past participle is **chosen**.

chord *noun* chords The /k/ sound is spelt **ch** in **chord**.

chronology *noun* The /k/ sound is spelt **ch** in **chronology**.

circle *noun* circles There is **le** at the end of **circle**.

circumference *noun* circumferences The /s/ sound is spelt with a **c** in **circumference**. Do not forget the **ence** at the end.

circumscribe *verb* circumscribes, circumscribing, circumscribed The /s/ sound is spelt with a **c** in **circumscribe**.

circumstance *noun* circumstances

city *noun* cities The plural of **city** is **cities**.

civilization *noun* civilizations

claw *noun* claws

claw *verb* claws, clawing, clawed

climb *verb* climbs, climbing, climbed There is a silent **b** at the end of **climb**.

climb *noun* climbs

clothes *plural noun* **Clothes** is plural and ends in **es**.

coefficient *noun* coefficients The ending of **coefficient** is spelt **cient**.

collaboration *noun* The ending of **collaboration** is spelt **tion**. Do not forget to double the **l**.

colonel *noun* colonels The /ɜː/ sound in **colonel** is spelt **olo**.

colour *noun* colours The /ə/ sound is spelt **our** in **colour**.

A
B
C
D
E
F
G
H
I
J
K
L
M
N
O
P
Q
R
S
T
U
V
W
X
Y
Z

A
B
C
D
E
F
G
H
I
J
K
L
M
N
O
P
Q
R
S
T
U
V
W
X
Y
Z

colour *verb* colours, colouring, coloured

column *noun* columns There is a silent **n** at the end of **column**.

committee *noun* committees **Committee** has a double **m**, a double **t** and a double **e**.

communication *noun* communications The ending of **communication** is spelt **tion**.

competition *noun* competitions The ending of **competition** is spelt **tion**.

complement *noun* complements

complete *verb* completes, completing, completed **Complete** ends with **ete**.

completely *adverb* **Complete** + **ly** = **completely**. Don't forget to keep the **e** after the **t**.

completion *noun*

compliment *noun* compliments Do not confuse this with **complement**.

comprehension *noun*

conceal *verb* conceals, concealing, concealed

conceive *verb* conceives, conceiving, conceived The /iː/ sound is spelt **ei** in **conceive**.

concentrate *verb* concentrates, concentrating, concentrated

confidential *adjective*

conker *noun* conkers Be careful, this sounds the same as **conquer**.

conquer *verb* conquers, conquering, conquered The /k/ sound is spelt **qu** in the middle of **conquer**.

conscience *noun*

conscious *adjective*

consciousness *noun* **Conscious**ness has **sci** in the middle.

consequence *noun* consequences There is an **e** after the **s** in **consequence**.

contraception *noun* The ending of **contraception** is spelt **tion**.

contribution *noun* contributions The ending of **contribution** is spelt **tion**.

correspondence *noun* There is a double **r** in **correspondence**.

cough *verb* coughs, coughing, coughed

cough *noun* coughs The end of **cough** is spelt **ough**.

couldn't Couldn't = **could** + **not**. Add an **apostrophe** between the **n** and the **t**.

courage *noun*

courageous *adjective*

creak *noun* creaks

creak *verb* creaks, creaking, creaked

creaky *adjective* The /iː/ sound in the middle of **creaky** is spelt **ea**.

creature *noun* creatures

creep *verb* creeps, creeping, crept The past tense of **creep** is **crept**. Do not add **ed**.

critic *noun* critics

cry *verb* cries, crying, cried The past tense of **cry** is **cried**.

cry *noun* cries

crystal *noun* crystals

cultivate *verb* cultivates, cultivating, cultivated There is a **c** at the start of **cultivate**.

cupboard *noun* cupboards

curiosity *noun* curiosities

currant *noun* currants

current *noun* currents

curtain *noun* curtains

cylinder *noun* cylinders The beginning of **cylinder** is spelt **cyl**.

Dd

daughter *noun* daughters The /ɔː/ sound is spelt **augh** in daughter.

dear *adjective* dearer, dearest

decametre *noun* The /k/ sound is spelt with a **c** in **decametre**. Do not forget the **re** at the end.

deceive *verb* deceives, deceiving, deceived **Deceive** ends with **eive**.

decide *verb* decides, deciding, decided There is a **c** in the middle of **decide**.

decimal *noun* decimals

decision *noun* decisions Remember that **decision** begins with **dec**, there is an **i** after the **c** and the ending is spelt **sion**.

deer *noun* deer

definite *adjective* There is an **i** before and after the **n** in **definite**.

definitely *adverb, interjection* **Definitely** = **definite** + **ly**. There is an **i** on both sides of the **n** in **definitely**.

delicious *adjective*

dense *adjective* There is no **c** in **dense**.

densely *adverb*

dependant *noun* dependants Choose the right word! **Dependant** is a noun; **dependent** is an adjective. *This kind of lifestyle suits somebody with no dependants. The industry is dependent on funding.*

dependence *noun* There is no **a** in **dependence**. Do not forget the **ce** at the end.

dependent *adjective*

descend *verb* descends, descending, descended The /s/ sound is spelt **sc** in **descend**.

describe *verb* describes, describing, described **Describe** begins with **des**.

desert *noun* deserts

desert *verb* deserts, deserting, deserted

design *noun* designs

design *verb* designs, designing, designed There is a silent **g** in **design**.

desperate *adjective* There is an **e** in the middle of **desperate**.

desperately *adverb*

dessert *noun* desserts

determine *verb* determines, determining, determined There is only one **t** in **determine**.

develop *verb* develops, developing, developed There is no **e** at the end of **develop**.

development *noun* developments There is only one **p** and one **l** in **development**.

dew *noun* Be careful, this sounds the same as **due**.

diamond *noun* diamonds There is an **a** in **diamond**.

dictionary *noun* dictionaries

didn't Didn't = did + not. Add an **apostrophe** between the **n** and the **t**.

die *verb* dies, dying, died Change the **ie** to **y** and add **ing** to make **dying**.

difference *noun* differences

different *adjective* Remember, there are two **fs**, an **er** and it ends in **ent**; there is no **a**.

digital *adjective* There is a **g** in **digital**.

dine *verb* dines, dining, dined

diner *noun* diners

dinner *noun* dinners

dinosaur *noun* dinosaurs

disappear *verb* disappears, disappearing, disappeared Remember, **disappear** is spelt with a single **s** and a double **p**.

disappoint *verb* disappoints, disappointing, disappointed Remember, **disappoint** is spelt with a single **s** and a double **p**.

disappointment *noun*

discuss *verb* discusses, discussing, discussed

disease *noun* diseases

disguise *verb* disguises, disguising, disguised

disguise *noun* disguises

disinterested *adjective*

disperse *verb* disperses, dispersing, dispersed There is an **i** after the **d** in **disperse**.

dissent *verb*, *noun*

distress *verb* distresses, distressing, distressed

diversity *noun* There is no **a** in **diversity**.

do *verb* does, doing, did, done The past tense of **do** is **did** and the past participle is **done**. *I did my work earlier. All my homework is done.*

doesn't Doesn't = does + not. Add an **apostrophe** between the **n** and the **t**.

dolphin *noun* dolphins

don't Don't = do + not. Add an **apostrophe** between the **n** and the **t**.

doubt *noun* doubts There is a silent **b** in **doubt**.

doubt *verb* doubts, doubting, doubted

dough *noun* The /əʊ/ sound is spelt **ough** in **dough**.

draft *noun* drafts

draft *verb* drafts, drafting, drafted

draught *noun* draughts Choose the right word! A **draught** is a current of air. A **draft** is a first version of something, and to **draft** something means to make a first version of it.

draw *verb* draws, drawing, drew, drawn The past tense of **draw** is **drew**.

drive *verb* drives, driving, drove, driven The past tense of **drive** is **drove** and the past participle is **driven**.

drive *noun* drives

driver *noun* drivers

due *adjective*, *adverb* Be careful, this sounds the same as **dew**.

duplication *noun* The ending of **duplication** is spelt **tion**.

Ee

eager *adjective*

eagerly *adverb*

early *adverb*, *adjective* earlier, earliest The /ɜː/ sound in **early** is spelt **ear**.

earn *verb* earns, earning, earned **Earn** begins with **ear**.

earth *noun* earths The /ɜː/ sound is spelt **ear** in **earth**.

east *noun*, *adjective*, *adverb* You use a capital **E** for **the East**, when you are talking about China, Japan, etc.

echo *noun* echoes

echo *verb* echoes, echoing, echoed There is no **e** in **echoing**.

ecstasy *noun* ecstasies **Ecstasy** ends with **asy**; not many words end with this pattern.

effect *noun* effects

A B C D E F G H I J K L M N O P Q R S T U V W X Y Z

A B C D E F G H I J K L M N O P Q R S T U V W X Y Z

effectively *adverb* Do not forget to double the **f** in **effectively**.

either *determiner, pronoun, adverb, conjunction*

electricity *noun*

electronically *adverb*

eligible *adjective*

ellipse *noun* ellipses Do not forget to double the **l** in **ellipse**.

ellipsoid *noun* ellipsoids Do not forget to double the **l** in **ellipsoid**.

embarrass *verb* embarrasses, embarrassing, embarrassed There is a double **r** and a double **s** in **embarrass**.

emigrate *verb* emigrates, emigrating, emigrated There is only one **m** in **emigrate**.

emperor *noun* emperors

engine *noun* engines

engineer *noun* engineers

enough *determiner, noun, adverb* The end of **enough** is spelt **ough**.

enquire *verb* enquires, enquiring, enquired

enquiry *noun* enquiries

envelope *noun* envelopes

environment *noun* environments There is a silent **n** in **environment**.

equally *adverb* Don't forget to double the **l** in **equally**.

equation *noun* equations The ending of **equation** is spelt **tion**.

evaluate *verb* evaluates, evaluating, evaluated There is only one **l** in **evaluate**.

every *determiner* Every has **er** in the middle, **ev-er-y**.

everyone *pronoun* Everyone has **er** in the middle, **ev-er-yone**.

exaggerate *verb* exaggerates, exaggerating, exaggerated

exaggeration *noun*

exceed *verb* exceeds, exceeding, exceeded The /s/ sound is spelt with a **c** in **exceed**.

except *preposition* The /s/ sound is spelt with a **c** in **except**.

exception *noun* exceptions

excite *verb* excites, exciting, excited The /s/ sound is spelt with a **c** in **excite**.

excitement *noun* excitements To make this word from **excite**, add **ment**. Keep the **e** at the end of **excite**.

exercise *noun* exercises There is no **c** after the **x** in **exercise**.

exercise *verb* exercises, exercising, exercised

explicit *adjective*

explosion *noun* explosions

express *noun* expresses

express *verb* expresses, expressing, expressed

extraordinary *adjective*

extreme *noun* extremes Extreme ends with **eme**.

extremely *adverb*

Ff

factor *noun* factors Do not forget the **or** at the end of **factor**.

fall *verb* falls, falling, fell, fallen The past tense of **fall** is **fell** and the past participle is **fallen**.

farther *adverb, adjective* Choose the right word! **Farther** means at a greater distance. Someone's **father** is their male parent.

fascinate *verb* fascinates, fascinating, fascinated The /s/ sound in **fascinate** is spelt **sc**.

fate *noun* fates

father *noun* fathers

favour *noun* favours

favour *verb* favours, favouring, favoured

favourite *noun* favourites There is an **ou** in the middle of **fav-ou-rite**.

feat *noun* feats Be careful, this sounds the same as **feet**.

feature *noun* features The /iː/ sound is spelt **ea** in **feature**.

feel *verb* feels, feeling, felt The past tense of **feel** is **felt**.

feet *noun* Be careful, this sounds the same as **feat**.

fete *noun* fetes Choose the right word! A **fete** is an outdoor entertainment with stalls. **Fate** is a power that is thought to make things happen.

fiction *noun* fictions

fictitious *adjective*

field *noun* fields The /iː/ sound in **field** is spelt ie.

field *verb* fields, fielding, fielded

fiendish *adjective*

fiendishly *adverb*

fierce *adjective* fiercer, fiercest

fight *noun* fights

fight *verb* fights, fighting, fought The past tense of **fight** is **fought**.

finally *adverb* Finally = final + ly. Don't forget to double the **l**.

finish *verb* finishes, finishing, finished There is only one **n** in **finish**.

flavour *noun* flavours

flavour *verb* flavours, flavouring, flavoured

flee *verb* flees, fleeing, fled

flour *noun*

flower *noun* flowers

flower *verb* flowers, flowering, flowered

flu *noun*

flue *noun* flues

fly *verb* flies, flying, flew, flown
The past tense of is **fly** is **flew**, and the past participle is **flown**.

fly *noun* flies

for *preposition, conjunction*
Be careful, this sounds the same as **fore**.

forcible *adjective*

fore *adjective, noun*

foreign *adjective*

forever *adverb*

formula *noun* formulas, formulae

fountain *noun* fountains

frantic *adjective*

frantically *adverb*
Frantic + ally = **frantically**.

frequency *noun* frequencies
There is no **a** in **frequency**.

frequent *verb* frequents, frequenting, frequented

friend *noun* friends There is an **i** before the **e** in **friend**.

fright *noun* frights The /aɪ/ sound is spelt **igh** in **fright**.

frighten *verb* frightens, frightening, frightened There is **ten** in the middle of **frightening**.

fruit *noun* fruit or fruits The /uː/ sound is spelt **ui** in **fruit**.

furious *adjective*

Gg

gateau *noun* gateaux The plural of **gateau** is **gateaux**.

genuine *adjective*

geometry *noun* Do not forget the **ome** in the middle of **geometry**.

germinate *verb* germinates, germinating, germinated

ghost *noun* ghosts There is a silent **h** after the **g** in **ghost**.

giant *noun* giants

glaciation *noun* The /s/ sound is spelt with a **c**, and the ending is spelt **tion** in **glaciation**.

glamorous *adjective*

globalisation *noun* The ending of **globalisation** is spelt **tion**.

glorious *adjective*

gloriously *adverb*

gnarled *adjective* There is a silent **g** at the start of **gnarled**.

gnash *verb* gnashes, gnashing, gnashed There is a silent **g** at the start of **gnash**.

gnat *noun* gnats

gnaw *verb* gnaws, gnawing, gnawed There is a silent **g** at the start of **gnaw**.

gnome *noun* gnomes

goddess *noun* goddesses There is a double **d** in the middle of **goddess**.

government *noun* governments

grammar *noun* grammars Grammar ends in **ar**.

growth *noun* Don't forget the **w** after the **o** in **growth**.

guarantee *noun* guarantees

guarantee *verb* guarantees, guaranteeing, guaranteed

guard *verb* guards, guarding, guarded

guard *noun* guards There is a silent **u** after the **g** in **guard**.

guess *noun* guesses There is a silent **u** after the **g** in **guess**.

guess *verb* guesses, guessing, guessed

Hh

hadn't Hadn't = had + not. Add an **apostrophe** between the **n** and the **t**.

half *noun* halves The plural of **half** is **halves**.

handkerchief *noun* handkerchiefs

handsome *adjective* handsomer, handsomest

happiness *noun*

harass *verb* harasses, harassing, harassed There is only one **r** in the middle of **harass**.

hasn't Hasn't = has + not. Add an **apostrophe** between the **n** and the **t**.

haughty *adjective* haughtier, haughtiest

haunt *verb* haunts, haunting, haunted

haven't Have + not = haven't. Add an **apostrophe** between the **n** and the **t**.

hear *verb* hears, hearing, heard The past tense of **hear** is **heard**.

he'd He'd = he + would or he + had. Add an **apostrophe** between the **e** and the **d**.

height *noun* heights The /aɪ/ sound is spelt **eigh** in **height**.

he'll He'll = he + will. Add an **apostrophe** between the **e** and the **ll**.

herbicide *noun* herbicides The /s/ sound is spelt with a **c** in **herbicide**.

here *adverb* Be careful, this sounds the same as **hear**.

hero *noun* heroes The plural of **hero** is **heroes**.

hers *pronoun* There is no apostrophe in **hers**.

Jj: Try also words beginning with **ge-**, **gi-**, or **gy-** Kk: Try also words beginning with **c-**, **ch-**, or **qu-**

A
B
C
D
E
F
G
H
I
J
K
L
M
N
O
P
Q
R
S
T
U
V
W
X
Y
Z

he's He's = he + is. Add an **apostrophe** between the **e** and the **s**.

his *determiner, pronoun* There is no apostrophe in **his**.

hole *noun* holes

honour *noun* honours

honour *verb* honours, honouring, honoured

honourable *adjective*

horizon *noun* horizons

howl *noun* howls

howl *verb* howls, howling, howled

humorous *adjective* There is no **u** in the middle of **humorous**.

humour *noun* There is a **ou** in **humour**.

hurt *verb* hurts, hurting, hurt The past tense of **hurt** is also **hurt**. Don't add **ed**.

hurtful *adjective*

hypotenuse *noun* hypotenuses Don't forget the **ten** in the middle of **hypotenuse**.

hypothesis *noun* hypotheses The plural of **hypothesis** is **hypotheses**.

Ii

I'd I'd = I + would or had. Add an **apostrophe** between the **I** and the **d**.

I'll I'll = I + will. Add an **apostrophe** between the **I** and the **ll**.

illegible *adjective*

illuminations *plural noun*

I'm I'm = I + am. Add an **apostrophe** between the **I** and the **m**.

imagination *noun* imaginations

immediate *adjective*

immediately *adverb*

immigration *noun* The ending of **immigration** is spelt **tion**. Do not forget to double the **m**.

implicit *adjective* The /s/ sound is spelt with a **c** in **implicit**.

impossible *adjective*

independent *adjective*

independently *noun*

infectious *adjective*

inferior *noun* inferiors

inferiority *noun*

infinitesimal *adjective* Don't forget the **tes** in the middle of **infinitesimal**.

inquire *verb* inquires, inquiring, inquired

inquiry *noun* inquiries Do not confuse this word with **enquiry**.

interest *verb* interests, interesting, interested

interest *noun* interests There is an **er** in the middle of **interest**.

interpretation *noun* interpretations The ending of **interpretation** is spelt **tion**. Do not forget the **ret** in the middle.

interrupt *verb* interrupts, interrupting, interrupted There is a double **r** in the middle of **interrupt**.

irreducible *adjective* There is a double **r** in **irreducible**, and do not forget the **ible** at the end.

irregular *adjective* There is a double **r** in **irregular**.

irrelevent *adjective*

island *noun* islands There is a silent **s** at the beginning of **island**.

isle *noun* isles Chose the right word! An **isle** is an island. An **aisle** is a passage in a church or cinema.

isn't Isn't = is + not. Add an **apostrophe** between the **n** and the **t**.

isosceles *adjective* There is **scel** in the middle of **isosceles**.

it'll It'll = it + will. Add an **apostrophe** between the **t** and the **ll**.

its *determiner, pronoun* Choose the right word! **Its** means belonging to something, *The dog ate its dinner hungrily*; **it's** is a contraction of **it is**, *It's a bit too late to go to the cinema.*

it's It's = it + is or it + has. Add an **apostrophe** between the **t** and the **s**.

I've I've = I + have. Add an **apostrophe** between the **I** and the **ve**.

Jj

jealous *adjective*

jealously *adverb*

journey *noun* journeys Just add **s** to make the plural **journeys**.

journey *verb* journeys, journeying, journeyed

judgement *noun* judgements There is **dge** in the middle of **judgement**.

juice *noun* juices Juice is a tricky word to spell: the /u:/ sound is spelt **ui** and the /s/ sound is spelt with a **c**.

Kk

keep *verb* keeps, keeping, kept The past tense of **keep** is **kept**.

kernel *noun* kernels Do not confuse this word with **colonel**.

key *noun* keys

kilogram *noun* kilograms There is only one **m** in **kilogram**.

kilometre *noun* kilometres Do not forget the **re** at the end of **kilometre**.

Kk: Try also words beginning with **c-**, **ch-**, or **qu-**

knead *verb* kneads, kneading, kneaded

knife *noun* knives **Knife** has a silent **k** at the beginning. The plural of **knife** is **knives**.

knock *verb* knocks, knocking, knocked **Knock** has a silent **k** at the beginning.

knock *noun* knocks

knot *noun* knots

knot *verb* knots, knotting, knotted There is a silent **k** at the start of **knot**. Choose the right word! A **knot** is a place where a piece of string or rope is twisted round. **Not** is used to show that something is negative, e.g. *Samir was not happy.*

knowledge *noun* **Knowledge** has a silent **k** at the beginning.

Ll

language *noun* languages

laugh *verb* laughs, laughing, laughed

laugh *noun* laughs

laughter *noun*

launch *verb* launches, launching, launched

launch *noun* launches

lay *verb* lays, laying, laid The past tense of **lay** is **laid**.

lead *verb* leads, leading, led The past tense of **lead** is **led**.

lead *noun* leads

league *noun* leagues

leakage *noun*

leap *noun* leaps

leap *verb* leaps, leaping, leapt or leaped The past tense of **leap** is **leapt** or **leaped**.

leave *verb* leaves, leaving, left The past tense of **leave** is **left**.

leisure *noun* There is an **i** in **leisure**.

length *noun* lengths Do not forget the **g** after the **n** in **length**.

lenient *adjective*

let's *verb* **Let's** = **let** + **us**. Add an apostrophe between the **t** and the **s**.

licence *noun* licences

license *verb* licenses, licensing, licensed

lie *verb* lies, lying, lied The past tense of **lie** meaning **to tell an untruth** is **lied**. When **lie** means **lie down**, the past tense is **lay** and the past participle is **lain**.

lie *noun* lies

lightning *noun* Lightning has no **e** in the middle!

likeable *adjective*

linear *adjective* Do not forget the **ear** at the end of **linear**.

litre *noun* litres Do not forget the **re** at the end of **litre**.

load *noun* loads

load *verb* loads, loading, loaded

locus *noun* loci The plural of **locus** is **loci**.

logarithm *noun* logarithms There is an **i** after the **r** in **logarithm**, and no vowel between the **h** and the **m**.

longitude *noun* There is an **i** in the middle of **longitude**.

loose *adjective* looser, loosest This word sounds like **moose**.

lose *verb* loses, losing, lost The past tense of **lose** is **lost**.

lot *noun* lots **A lot** is two words, not one. Keep them apart!

Mm

machine *noun* machines

magician *noun* magicians

magnificent *adjective*

magnificently *adverb*

make *verb* makes, making, made The past tense of **make** is **made**.

malicious *adjective*

malware *noun* The /eə/ sound is spelt **are** at the end of **malware**.

manageable *adjective* Keep the **e** in the middle of **manageable**.

marriage *noun* marriages

marvellous *adjective* There is a double **l** in **marvellous**.

marvellously *adverb*

mean *verb* means, meaning, meant The past tense of **mean** is **meant**.

measure *noun* measures

measure *verb* measures, measuring, measured The ending of **measure** is spelt **sure**.

mechanism *noun* mechanisms The /k/ sound is spelt **ch** in **mechanism**. Remember, there is no vowel between the **s** and the **m** at the end.

medicine *noun* medicines

medieval *adjective* There is **al** at the end of **medieval**.

medium *noun* media or mediums There is an **i** after the **d** in **medium**.

meet *verb* meets, meeting, met The past tense of **meet** is **met**.

mention *verb* mentions, mentioning, mentioned The ending of **mention** is spelt **tion**.

mention *noun* mentions

meridian *noun* meridians There is only one **r** in **meridian**.

metaphor *noun* metaphors The /f/ sound is spelt **ph** in **metaphor**.

A
B
C
D
E
F
G
H
I
J
K
L
M
N
O
P
Q
R
S
T
U
V
W
X
Y
Z

migration *noun* The ending of **migration** is spelt **tion**.

millilitre *noun* millilitres Do not forget the **re** at the end of **millilitre**.

millimetre *noun* millimetres Do not forget the **re** at the end of **millimetre**.

millionaire *noun* millionaires Double up the **l** in **millionaire** but the **n** stays single.

minute *noun* minutes There is no **mini** in **minute**. A good way to remember this is **min + ute**.

minutely *adverb*

mischievous *adjective*

misspell *verb* misspells, misspelling, misspelt or misspelled

mnemonic *noun* mnemonics There is a silent **m** at the beginning of **mnemonic**.

mosquito *noun* mosquitoes

mountainous *adjective*

mourner *noun*

multiplication *noun* multiplications The ending of **multiplication** is spelt **tion**.

muscle *noun* muscles The /s/ sound is spelt **sc** in **muscle**.

muscle *verb* muscles, muscling, muscled

museum *noun* museums

musician *noun* musicians

mysterious *adjective*

Nn

necessary *adjective* There is one **c** and a double **s** in **necessary**. Do not forget the **ary** at the end.

need *verb* needs, needing, needed

need *noun* needs

neighbour *noun* neighbours The /eɪ/ sound is spelt **eigh** at the start of **neighbour**. Do not forget the **our** at the end.

neighbouring *adjective*

neighbourhood *noun* neighbourhoods

neither *determiner, pronoun, conjunction*

no one *pronoun* No one is two separate words.

not *adverb*

notably *adverb*

noticeable *adjective*

nucleated *adjective* There is no **r** in **nucleated**.

nuisance *noun* nuisances There is a **ui** in the middle of **nuisance**.

Oo

oblige *verb* obliges, obliging, obliged

ocean *noun* oceans

of *preposition*

off *adverb, preposition*

onomatopoeia *noun* Remember: **ono** at the start and **oeia** at the end of **onomatopoeia**.

our *determiner* Be careful, this sounds the same as **hour**.

ours *pronoun* There is no apostrophe in **ours**: *Those sweets are ours.*

outrageous *adjective*

oxygen *noun*

Pp

pail *noun* pails

pain *noun* pains

pain *verb* pains, paining, pained

pair *noun* pairs

pale *adjective* paler, palest

pane *noun* panes

parallel *adjective* Remember, one **r** and a double **l** in the middle of **parallel**.

parallelogram *noun* parallelograms Remember, one **r** and a double **l** before the **e** in **parallelogram**, but only one **l** after the **e**.

parliament *noun* parliaments

pass *verb* passes, passing, passed Choose the right word! **Passed** is the past tense of **pass**; if you go **past** something, you go near it and then continue moving until it is behind you, e.g. *We passed the house. Carry on past the Post Office then turn right.*

pass *noun* passes

past *noun, adjective, preposition* Do not confuse this word with **passed.**

pay *verb* pays, paying, paid The past tense of **pay** is **paid**.

peace *noun*

peak *noun* peaks

peak *verb* peaks, peaking, peaked

peal *verb* peals, pealing, pealed

peal *noun* peals

pear *noun* pears

peculiar *adjective*

pedal *noun* pedals

pedal *verb* pedals, pedalling, pedalled

peddle *verb* peddles, peddling, peddled

peek *noun* peeks

peek *verb* peeks, peeking, peeked

peel *noun* peels

peel *verb* peels, peeling, peeled

peer *verb* peers, peering, peered

peer *noun* peers

people *noun* peoples

perceive *verb* perceives, perceiving, perceived

perimeter *noun* perimeters Remember the **er** at the end of **perimeter**.

permanent *adjective*

persistence *noun* persistences There is no **a** in **persistence**. Do not forget the **sis** in the middle.

persistent *adjective* persistent There is no **a** in **persistent**. Do not forget the **sis** in the middle.

person *noun* persons or people

personification *noun* The ending of **personification** is spelt **tion**, and there is only one **n** in the middle.

persuade *verb* persuades, persuading, persuaded

pesticide *noun* pesticides Remember, there is **ici** in the middle of **pesticide**.

piece *noun* pieces Remember, you can have a **pie**ce of **pie**!

piece *verb* pieces, piecing, pieced

pier *noun* piers

plain *adjective* plainer, plainest

plain *noun* plains

pleasure *noun* pleasures

poisonous *adjective*

politician *noun* politicians

polygon *noun* polygons There is only one **n** in **polygon**, and no **e** at the end.

pompous *adjective*

pompously *adverb*

population *noun* populations The ending of **population** is spelt **tion**.

possess *verb* possesses, possessing, possessed

possession *noun* possessions

possibility *noun* possibilities There is no **a** in **possibility**. Do not forget to double the **s**.

potato *noun* potatoes Add **es** for the plural, **potatoes**.

practice *noun* practices Do not confuse this word with **practise**.

practise *verb* practises, practising, practised Choose the right word! **Practise** is a verb and **practice** is a noun. *Kirendeep was practising her lines for the school play. Zola forgot to go to orchestra practice.*

pray *verb* prays, praying, prayed

precious *adjective*

preparation *noun* preparations

presence *noun*

prey *verb* preys, preying, preyed Be careful, this sounds the same as **pray**.

principal *noun* principals

principally *adverb*

principle *noun* principles

prise *verb* prises, prising, prised

prism *noun* prisms There is no vowel between the **s** and the **m** in **prism**.

prize *noun* prizes

prize *verb* prizes, prizing, prized Choose the right word! A **prize** (noun) is something that you win in a competition. To **prize** (verb) something means to value it highly. To **prise** (verb) something open means to open it using force.

probably *adverb* Probably = probable + y.

process *noun* processes

process *verb* processes, processing, processed

professor *noun* professors There is one **f** and a double **s** in **professor**.

profit *noun* profits

profit *verb* profits, profiting, profited

program *noun* programs

program *verb* programs, programming, programmed

programme *noun* programmes

pronounce *verb* pronounces, pronouncing, pronounced

pronunciation *noun* pronunciations

propaganda *noun* There is no **e** or **r** in **propaganda**.

prophet *noun* prophets Be careful, this sounds the same as **profit**.

proprietary *adjective* There is **ary** at the end of **proprietary**.

protractor *noun* protractors There is **or** at the end of **protractor**.

put *verb* puts, putting, put Choose the right word! To **put** something somewhere is to place it there. To **putt** a ball is to tap it gently.

putt *verb* putts, putting, putted

putt *noun* putts

pyramid *noun* pyramids The /ɪ/ sound is spelt with a **y** at the start of **pyramid**.

Qq

quadrilateral *noun* quadrilaterals There is only one **t** in **quadrilateral**.

qualitative *adjective* There is **tat** before the **ive** in **qualitative**.

quantitative *adjective* There is **tat** before the **ive** in **quantitative**.

Rr: Try also words beginning with **rh-** or **wr-**   Ss: Try also words beginning with **ce-, ci-** or **sc-**

A B C D E F G H I J K L M N O P Q R S T U V W X Y Z

quay *noun* quays This sounds like **key**.

quota *noun* quotas There is **ta** at the end of **quota**.

quotient *noun* quotients The end of **quotient** is spelt **tient**.

Rr

rain *verb* rains, raining, rained

read *verb* reads, reading, read The past tense of **read** is the same spelling but rhymes with **red**.

realize *verb* realizes, realizing, realized You can spell this with **ize** or **ise**.

really *adverb* There is double **l** in the middle of **really**.

realm *noun* realms There is **ea** in **realm**.

receipt *noun* receipts There is an **ei** in the middle and a silent **p** in **receipt**.

receive *verb* receives, receiving, received The /iː/ sound is spelt **ei** in **receive**.

region *noun* regions There is a **g** in **region**.

reign *verb* reigns, reigning, reigned The /eɪ/ sound is spelt **eig** in **reign**. Don't forget the silent **g**.

reign *noun* reigns

rein *noun* reins Be careful, this sounds the same as **reign**.

reiterate *verb*

religion *noun* religions There is a **g** in **religion**.

religious *adjective*

remember *verb* remembers, remembering, remembered To make the past tense, **remember + ed, remembered**.

repetition *noun* repetitions There is only one p, and the ending is spelt **tion** in **repetition**.

resign *verb* resigns, resigning, resigned There is a silent **g** before the **n** in **resign**.

rewrite *verb* rewrites, rewriting, rewrote, rewritten The past tense is **rewrote** and the past participle is **rewritten**.

rhomboid *noun* rhomboids There is a silent **h** after the **r** in **rhomboid**.

rhombus *noun* rhombuses There is a silent **h** after the **r** in **rhombus**.

rhyme *noun* rhymes

rhyme *verb* rhymes, rhyming, rhymed There is a silent **h** after the **r** in **rhyme**.

rhythm *noun* rhythms Try learning the phrase 'rhythm helps your two hips move' to spell **rhythm**.

ride *verb* rides, riding, rode, ridden The past tense of **ride** is **rode** and the past participle is **ridden**.

ride *noun* rides

ridiculous *adjective*

ridiculously *adverb*

right *noun* rights

right *verb* rights, righting, righted

rightfully *adverb*

ring *noun* rings

ring *verb* rings, ringing, rang, rung The past tense is **rang** and the past participle is **rung**.

rite *noun* rites

road *noun* roads

roof *noun* roofs The plural of **roof** is **roofs**.

root *noun* roots

root *verb* roots, rooting, rooted

rough *adjective* rougher, roughest

roughness *noun*

route *noun* routes

row *noun* rows

row *verb* rows, rowing, rowed

Ss

sac *noun* sacs

sack *noun* sacks

sack *verb* sacks, sacking, sacked

sail *noun* sails

sail *verb* sails, sailing, sailed

sale *noun* sales

satellite *noun* satellites

saw *noun* saws Choose the right word! A **saw** is a tool for cutting wood. If a part of your body is **sore**, it hurts.

say *verb* says, saying, said The past tense of **say** is **said**.

scene *noun* scenes Choose the right word! A **scene** is a place or part of a play. **Seen** is the past participle of **see**.

science *noun*

scissors *plural noun* There is an **sc** at the start of **scissors**.

scream *noun* screams

scream *verb* screams, screaming, screamed The /iː/ sound is spelt **ea** in **scream**.

sea *noun* seas

see *verb* sees, seeing, saw, seen The past tense of **see** is **saw**. The /ɔː/ sound is spelt **aw** in **saw**.

seize *verb* seizes, seizing, seized The /iː/ sound is spelt **ei** in **seize**.

self *noun* selves Change the **f** to **ves** to make the plural **selves**.

sell *verb* sells, selling, sold The past tense of **sell** is **sold**.

send *verb* sends, sending, sent The past tense of **send** is **sent**.

Ss: Try also words beginning with **ce-**, **ci-** or **sc-**

separate *verb* separates, separating, separated There is an **a** in the middle of **separate**.

separation *noun*

sequence *noun* sequences

sequence *verb* sequences, sequencing, sequenced There is no **a** in **sequence**.

serial *noun* serials Do not confuse this word with **cereal**.

series *noun* series

serious *adjective*

seriously *adverb*

settlement *noun* settlements There is **le** in the middle of **settlement**.

sew *verb* sews, sewing, sewed, sewn or sewed Choose the right word! To **sew** is to work with a needle and thread. To **sow** seed means to put it in the ground.

shake *verb* shakes, shaking, shook, shaken The past tense of **shake** is **shook** and the past participle is **shaken**.

shake *noun* shakes

she'd She'd = she + would or she + had. Don't forget to add an **apostrophe** between the **e** and the **d**.

sheep *noun* sheep The plural of **sheep** is **sheep**.

she'll She'll = she + will. Don't forget to add an **apostrophe** between the **e** and the **ll**.

shepherd *noun* shepherds There is a silent **h** in the middle of **shepherd**.

she's She's = she + is or she + has. Don't forget to add an apostrophe between the **e** and the **s**.

shearer *noun*

shield *noun* shields The /iː/ sound is spelt **ie** in **shield**.

shield *verb* shields, shielding, shielded

should *verb*

shoulder *noun* shoulders

shoulder *verb* shoulders, shouldering, shouldered

shriek *noun* shrieks

shriek *verb* shrieks, shrieking, shrieked

sigh *noun* sighs

sigh *verb* sighs, sighing, sighed

sight *noun* sights Be careful, this sounds the same as **site**.

sight *verb* sights, sighting, sighted

sign *noun* signs There is a silent **g** in **sign**.

sign *verb* signs, signing, signed

simile *noun* similes There is only one **m** in **simile**.

simulation *noun* simulations The ending of **simulation** is spelt **tion**.

simultaneous *adjective*

sincere *adjective* sincerer, sincerest

sing *verb* sings, singing, sang, sung The past tense of **sing** is **sang** and the past participle is **sung**.

site *noun* sites

site *verb* sites, siting, sited

sketch *noun* sketches

sketch *verb* sketches, sketching, sketched

society *noun* societies

soldier *noun* soldiers There is a **di** in **soldier**.

solemn *adjective* There is a silent **n** at the end of **solemn**.

something *pronoun* Something is made from **some** + **thing**. Don't forget the **e** in the middle.

sore *noun* sores Do not confuse this word with **saw**.

source *noun* sources

sourness *noun*

sow *verb* sows, sowing, sowed, sown The past participle of **sow** can be either **sown** or **sowed**. Do not confuse this word with **sew**.

spaghetti *noun* There is a silent **h** after the **g** in **spaghetti**. Don't forget to double the **t**.

sparsely *adverb*

species *noun* species

speed *noun* speeds

speed *verb* speeds, speeding, sped or speeded

sphere *noun* spheres The /f/ sound is spelt **ph** in **sphere**.

stair *noun* stairs

stake *noun* stakes

stake *verb* stakes, staking, staked Be careful, this sounds the same as **steak**.

stare *verb* stares, staring, stared

stare *noun* stares Do not confuse this word with **stair**.

stationary *adjective*

stationery *noun* Choose the right word! Stationery means paper and other writing materials. Remember there is an **e** in envelope and also in **stationery**.

steak *noun* steaks

steal *verb* steals, stealing, stole, stolen The past tense of **steal** is **stole** and the past participle is **stolen**.

steel *verb* steels, steeling, steeled

stomach *noun* stomachs

storage *noun* There is no **i** in **storage**.

straight *adjective* straighter, straightest

A B C D E F G H I J K L M N O P Q R S T U V W X Y Z

151

A
B
C
D
E
F
G
H
I
J
K
L
M
N
O
P
Q
R
S
T
U
V
W
X
Y
Z

strength *noun* strengths There is a **g** after the **n** in **strength**.

sty *noun* sties

stylus *noun* styluses There is **us** at the end of **stylus**.

substantial *adjective*

success *noun* successes There is a double **c** and a double **s** in **success**.

sudden *adjective* Do not forget to double the **d** in the middle of **sudden**.

sufficient *adjective*

suffragette *noun* suffragettes There is a **g** in **suffragette**. Do not forget to double the **f** and the **t**.

sum *noun* sums Do not confuse this word with **some**.

summarise *verb* summarises, summarising, summarised Do not forget to double the **m** in **summarise**. This can be spelt **ise** or **ize**.

superior *noun* superiors

surprise *noun* surprises There is an **r** after the **u** in **surprise**.

suspicious *adjective*

syllable *noun* syllables

symbol *noun* symbols The /ɪ/ sound is spelt with a **y** in **symbol**.

symmetry *noun* The /ɪ/ sound is spelt with a **y** in **symmetry**. Do not forget to double the **m**.

Tt

tail *noun* tails

tail *verb* tails, tailing, tailed

tale *noun* tales

team *noun* teams

tear *verb* tears, tearing, tore, torn The verb **tear** rhymes with **hair** and means to rip something.

The past tense of the verb **tear** is **tore** and the past participle is **torn**.

tear *noun* tears The noun **tear** rhymes with fear and is used to talk about the water that comes out of your eyes when you are upset.

technology *noun* technologies The /k/ sound is spelt **ch** in **technology**.

teem *verb* teems, teeming, teemed

tell *verb* tells, telling, told The past tense of **tell** is **told**.

temperature *noun* temperatures Do not forget the **er** in the middle of **temperature**.

template *noun* templates Do not forget the **ate** at the end of **template**.

tension *noun* tensions

tessellate *verb* tessellates, tessellating, tessellated Do not forget to double the **s** and the **l** in **tessellate**.

their *determiner* Be careful, this sounds the same as **they're** and **there**.

there *adverb* Be careful, this sounds the same as **they're** and **their**.

they *pronoun* The /eɪ/ sound is spelt **ey** in **they**.

they'd They'd = they + had or they + would. Do not forget to add an apostrophe between the **y** and the **d**.

they'll They'll = they + will. Do not forget to add an **apostrophe** between the **y** and the **ll**.

they're They're = they = are. Do not forget to add an **apostrophe** between the **y** and the **re**.

they've They + have = they've. Do not forget to add an **apostrophe** between the **y** and the **ve**.

think *verb* thinks, thinking, thought The past tense of **think**

is **thought**. The /ɔː/ sound is spelt **ough** in **thought**.

thorough *adjective* It is easy to confuse this word with **through**.

thoroughly *adverb*

though *conjunction, adverb* The /əʊ/ sound is spelt **ough** in **though**.

thought *noun* thoughts

thousand *noun*

through *adverb, preposition, adjective* The /uː/ sound is spelt **ough** in **through**.

throw *verb* throws, throwing, threw, thrown The past tense of **throw** is **threw** and the past participle is **thrown**.

throw *noun* throws

tire *verb* tires, tiring, tired

to *preposition, adverb* Be careful, this sounds the same as **too** and **two**.

toe *noun* toes

tomorrow *noun, adverb* There is one **m** and a double **r** in **tomorrow**.

tongue *noun* tongues

too *adverb*

tooth *noun* teeth The plural of **tooth** is **teeth**.

tourism *noun* There is no vowel between the **s** and the **m** in **tourism**.

tow *verb* tows, towing, towed

transformation *noun* transformations The ending of **transformation** is spelt **tion**.

trapezoid *noun* trapezoids There is only one **p** in **trapezoid**.

tread *verb* treads, treading, trod, trodden The past tense of **tread** is **trod** and the past participle is **trodden**.

treasure *noun* treasures

Ww: Try also words beginning with **wh-**

treasure *verb* treasures, treasuring, treasured

triumph *noun* triumphs

triumph *verb* triumphs, triumphing, triumphed

trough *noun* troughs The end of **trough** is spelt **ough**.

truly *adverb* Take the **e** off **true** and add **ly** to spell **truly**.

try *verb* tries, trying, tried The past tense of **try** is **tried**.

try *noun* tries

turn *verb* turns, turning, turned No need to double the **n** when you add **ing** or **ed** to **turn**.

turn *noun* turns

two *noun* twos

tyre *noun* tyres

Uu

uncomfortable *adjective*

unfair *adjective*

unfortunately *adverb* Start with **unfortunate** and add **ly**, **unfortunate** + **ly** = **unfortunately**.

uninterested *adjective* Choose the right word! **Uninterested** means not interested or bored and **disinterested** means impartial.

unique *adjective*

unnecessary *adjective*

untidily *adverb*

untidiness *noun*

until *preposition, conjunction* There is only one **l** in **until**.

upon *preposition* There is only one **p** in **upon**.

Vv

vaccinate *verb* vaccinates, vaccinating, vaccinated

vain *adjective* vainer, vainest

valuable *adjective*

vane *noun* vanes

vehicle *noun* vehicles

vein *noun* veins

very *adverb, adjective* There is only one **r** in **very**.

vicious *adjective*

villain *noun* villains

virtual *adjective* The /ɜː/ sound is spelt **ir** at the beginning of **virtual**.

vocabulary *noun* vocabularies

Ww

wail *verb* wails, wailing, wailed

wail *noun* wails

waist *noun* waists

wait *verb* waits, waiting, waited

wait *noun* waits

wary *adjective* warier, wariest

wasn't Wasn't = **was** + **not**. Do not forget to add an **apostrophe** between the **n** and the **t**.

waste *verb* wastes, wasting, wasted

waste *noun* wastes

watt *noun* watts

way *noun* ways

weak *adjective* weaker, weakest

wear *verb* wears, wearing, wore, worn

wearer *noun*

weary *adjective* wearier, weariest Do not confuse this word with **wary**.

weather *noun* Do not confuse this word with **whether**.

weather *verb* weather, weathering, weathered

weave *verb* weaves, weaving, wove, woven These are the correct forms if you mean **weave cloth**. If you mean **weave through crowds**, the past tense and participle are **weaved**.

we'd We'd = **we** + **had** or **we** + **would**. Do not forget to add an **apostrophe** between the **e** and the **d**.

week *noun* weeks

weigh *verb* weighs, weighing, weighed The /eɪ/ sound is spelt **eigh** in **weigh**.

weight *noun* weight

weight *verb* weights, weighting, weighted

weird *adjective* weirder, weirdest

weirdly *adverb* The /ɪə/ sound is spelt **ei** in **weird**.

weirdness *noun*

we'll We'll = **we** + **will** or **we** + **shall**. Do not forget to add an **apostrophe** between the **e** and the **ll**.

went *verb*

were *verb* Were is the past tense of **be**, used with **you/we/they**.

we're We're = **we** + **are**. Add an apostrophe between the **e** and the **r**.

we've We've = **we** + **have**. Do not forget to add an apostrophe between the **e** and the **ve**.

whale *noun* whales

what *determiner, pronoun* There is a silent **h** after the **w** in **what**.

where *adverb, conjunction*

whether *conjunction* Do not confuse this word with **weather**.

A B C D E F G H I J K L M N O P Q R S T U V W X Y Z

A
B
C
D
E
F
G
H
I
J
K
L
M
N
O
P
Q
R
S
T
U
V
W
X
Y
Z

which *determiner, pronoun* There is a silent **h** after the **w** in **which**.

whine *verb* whines, whining, whined

whine *noun* whines There is a silent **h** after the **w** in **whine**.

whisper *verb* whispers, whispering, whispered There is a silent **h** after the **w** in **whisper**.

whisper *noun* whispers

whistle *verb* whistles, whistling, whistled

whistle *noun* whistles

whole *noun* wholes Be careful, this sounds the same as **hole**.

who's Who's = who + is or has. Do not forget to add an apostrophe between the **o** and the **s**.

whose *adjective, pronoun* Do not confuse this word with **who's**, which is a contraction of who + **has** or **is**.

width *noun* width There is no **h** after the **w** in **width**.

wine *noun* wines Do not confuse this word with **whine**.

witch *noun* witches Do not confuse this word with **which**.

with *preposition* There is no **h** after the **w** in **with**.

wolf *noun* wolves The plural of **wolf** is **wolves**.

won't Won't is short for **will** + **not**. Do not forget to add an **apostrophe** between the **n** and the **t**.

wood *noun* woods

would *verb*

wouldn't Wouldn't = would + not. Do not forget to add an apostrophe between the **n** and the **t**.

wring *verb* wrings, wringing, wrung The past tense of **wring** is **wrung**. Do not forget the silent **w** before the **r**. Do not confuse this word with **ring**.

write *verb* writes, writing, wrote, written There is a silent **w** at the start of **write**. The past tense of **write** is **wrote** and the past participle is **written**.

Yy

yield *noun* yields

yield *verb* yields, yielding, yielded The /iː/ sound is spelt **ie** in **yield**.

you'd You'd can be short for **you** + **would** or **you** + **had**. Do not forget to add an **apostrophe** between the **u** and the **d**.

you'll You'll = **you** + **will**. Do not forget to add an **apostrophe** between the **u** and the **ll**.

your *determiner* Do not confuse this word with **you're**, which is a contraction of **you** + **are**.

you're You're = **you** + **are**. Do not forget to add an apostrophe between the **u** and the **re**. Do not confuse **you're** and **your**. You're means you are, e.g. *you're taller than me*. **Your** means belonging to the person you are talking to, e.g. *your house is on the same street as mine*.

you've You've = **you** + **have**. Do not forget to add an apostrophe between the **u** and the **v**.

A

abbreviations	95
abstract nouns	**6**
active voice	**38**
adjective phrases	**61**
adjectives	**11-13**, 29, 42, 44, 61, 118-121, 125
adverb phrases	**62**
adverbials	40, **45-46**, 60
adverbs	27, **41-44**, 57, 60, 62, 99, 121
agreement, noun-verb	**9**
agreement, subject-verb	**68**
-al	**136**
ampersands	**108**
-ant	**127**
antonyms	**87**
apostrophes	54, 82, **105-106**, 128-129
articles	**52-53**
auxiliary verbs	**23-26**, 31

B

'be'	16, **22**, **23**, 69
brackets	**102**
bullet points	**107**

C

capital letters	7, **94-95**, 100, 107
-cher	**128**
-cial	**127**
-cious	**127**
clauses	49, 58-59, **63-65**, 71, 98
cohesion	**90**
cohesive devices	41, 43, 46, **60**, **90**
collective nouns	**10**
colloquialism	**80**
colons	**100**, 107
commands	**66**, 96
commas	12, 64-65, **97-99**, 102
common nouns	**7**
comparative adjectives	**13**, **118-120**
complements	15-16, **69-70**
complex sentences	71
compound nouns	**9**
compound sentences	see 'multi-clause sentences'
concrete nouns	**5**
conjunctions	**58-59**, 60, 63, 71
connectives	42, 58, 60
consonants	**109**
contractions	**82**, 105, 128-129
coordinating conjunctions	**58**, 71
correcting written work	**91-92**
countable nouns	**8**

INDEX

D

dashes	**102**
defining relative clauses	**64**
definite article	**53**
demonstrative determiners	**54**
demonstrative pronouns	**49**
determiners	**52-55**
direct speech	82, **83**, 104
'do'	**24**

E

-ed	**116-117**
effective writing	**74-75**
-el	**136**
ellipses	**103**
emphasizers	**42**
-ent	**127**
-er	**118-119**, 124
-est	**118-119**
exclamation marks	**96**
exclamations	**66**, 96

F

fiction	72-73, 107
figurative language	85
finite verbs	**28**
first person	37, 47-48, 50, 67-68, **72**, 95
formal writing	6, 27, 39, 43, 51, 65, 73, **78-79**, 83, 84, 85, 102, 107
forward slash	**108**
fronted adverbials	**46**

full stops, future column

full stops	72, **94**, 107
future	17-22, 30-31, **37-38**

G

gradable adjectives	**13**

H

'have'	**24**
homographs	**131**
homophones	**130**
hyphen	**103**

I

indefinite article	**52**
indirect speech	see 'reported speech'
infinitives	28, **30**
inflections	see 'verb inflections'
informal writing	6, 37, 51, 75, 78, **80-81**, 82, 102
-ing	**115-116**
intensifiers	**42**
interrogative determiners	**54**
interrogative possessive determiner	54
interrogative pronouns	**50**
intransitive verbs	70
inverted commas	see 'speech marks'
irregular verbs	**18-22**, 117
it's/its	105, **129**

L

-le	**136**

INDEX

link verbs	**15-16**
lists	97, 100, 101, 102
long vowel sounds	**109-112**
-ly	44, **121**

M

main clauses	**63**, 66, 71, 98, 103
metaphorical language	85
mnemonics	**137**
modal verbs	**25-26**, 30, 31
modifying nouns	**9**
'more'	**119-120**
'most'	**119-120**
multi-clause sentences	**71**, 97-98

N

narrative voice	**72-73**
nominalization	**6**
non-defining relative clauses	**65**
non-finite verbs	**28**
non-gradable adjectives	**13**
non-standard English	**76-77**
noun phrase	11, 47, **61**
nouns	**5-10**, 29, 47, 52-53, 61, 69, 125

O

object	39, **69-70**
ou	**136**
ough	**135**
oxford comma	see 'serial comma'

P

paragraphs	89
parenthesis	65, **102**
parenthetic commas	**102**
participles	12, 28, **29**, 63
passive voice	23, **38-40**
past participles	12, 18-19, **29**
past perfect continuous tense	see 'past perfect progressive tense'
past perfect progressive tense	**36**
past perfect tense	**35**
past progressive tense	**35**
past tenses	17-22, 30-31, **34-36**, 116-117
perfect tenses	24, 33, 34, 35, 36, 38
person (1st/2nd/3rd)	47-48, 50, **72-73**
personal pronouns	**47**
phrasal verbs	**27-28**
phrases	**61-62**, 63
plural	8, 9, 10, 53, 55, 67-68, 74, 106, **113-114**, 130
possessive determiners	48, **53**
possessive pronouns	**48**
prefixes	87, 103, **122-123**
preposition phrases	**62**
prepositions	27, **56-57**, 62
present continuous tense	see 'progressive tense'

INDEX

present participles	12, **29**
present perfect continuous tense	see 'present perfect progressive tense'
present perfect progressive tense	**34**
present perfect tense	**33**
present progressive tense	23, **33**
present tenses	17-22, 30-31, **32-34**, 115-116
pronouns	**47-51**, 55, 64
proofreading	93
proper nouns	**7**, 95
punctuation marks	**94-108**

Q

question marks	83, **96**
question tags	**80**
questions	50, 66, 79, 96
quotations	103, **104**

R

reflexive pronouns	**50-51**
regular verbs	**17-18**
relative clauses	**64-65**
relative pronouns	**49**, 64, 65
reported speech	84

S

-s	**113-114**
second person	47-48, 50, 67-68, **72**
semicolons	**101**
sentence adverbs	**43**

sentences	28, **66**, **71**, 94
serial comma	**97**
silent letters	**132**
simple past tense	18-19, 20-22, **34**
simple present tense	20-22, **32**
single-clause sentences	**71**
singular	9, 10, 52, 67-68, **113**
soft c	**133**
soft g	**133**
speech marks	84, **104**
spelling tips	**137**
spelling word endings	**126-128**
standard English	**76-77**
statements	24, 66
subject	9, 17, 39-40, **66-68**, 69, 71
subordinate clauses	28, 59, **63-65**, 71, 98
subordinating conjunctions	**59**
suffixes	9, 12, 14, 44, 87, **124-5**
superlative adjectives	**13, 118-20**
synonyms	**86**

T

tenses	17, 28, **30-38**, 72
their/there/they're	**128**
third person	32, 47-48, 50, **73**
-tial	**127**

-tious	**127**
transitive verbs	**70**
tricky letters	**133-135**
-ture	**128**

U

uncountable nouns	**8**, 9, 53, 55, 74
underlining	**108**

V

verb inflections	14, **17-22**
verbs	9, **14-30**, 30-40, 45, 66-68, 70, 115-117, 125
voice	17, **38-39**
vowels	**109-112**

W

we're/were	**128**
who's/whose	**129**
word classes	**5**, 125
word endings – spelling	**126-128**
word families	**137**

Y

you're/your	**129**